A Place Called Simplicity

Claire Cloninger

HARVEST HOUSE PUBLISHERS
Eugene, Oregon 97402

A PLACE CALLED SIMPLICITY

Copyright © 1993 by Claire Cloninger
Published by Harvest House Publishers
Eugene, Oregon 97402

For Spike who said,
"Maybe we really should try it. . . ."

Acknowledgments

————— ❦ —————

My deep appreciation to . . .

My children, Curt, Andy, and Jenni, who are a constant source of inspiration.

My editor, Anne Christian Buchanan, who knows all there is to know 'bout birthin' books!

My friend Dale, who didn't want to write this book and thought I might.

My editor at Harvest House, Eileen Mason, who braved the backroads of Baldwin County to see for herself. ("Yes, Eileen, there really is a Juniper Landing!")

My prayer partners, Pam, Signa, Nancy, and Nancy, who have been the net beneath my trapeze.

My Cloninger, deGravelles, and Christ Church families, who make my life so much simpler just by being there.

Contents

———————— 🍎 ————————

———————— 🍎 ————————

Are You a Simplicity Seeker?

———————— ❦ ————————

Have you found yourself wondering more and more lately, *Why does my life have to be so complicated?*

Do you dread dealing with the chaotic contents of your work space? Your closet? Your checkbook? Your appointment calendar? Are there things you yearn to do and people you yearn to be with, but you can't seem to find the time for either? Or do you find yourself spending too much time doing things you don't really care about with people you don't really care for?

Do you already own more *things* than you can use, keep clean, or find storage space for—yet you seem to be constantly shopping for some new item that you "really need"? Are your finances in a tangle? Are your credit cards on overload? Do you find it difficult to stop working and worrying, even on off days and vacations?

Is your house a haven of tranquillity to which you can run at the end of the day, or does it feel as rushed and chaotic as the rest of the world? Do you feel your life is your own, or are you marching to the beat of someone else's drum? (Your parents? The Joneses? Madison Avenue?) Is your work challenging, exciting, rewarding? Or do you feel like you're on a treadmill going nowhere at a rapid pace?

Do you look back at your childhood with nostalgia and yearn for those days of simplicity and freedom? Do you ever just wish there was an exit door to all the hassle and headaches that have attached themselves to your life?

If even a few of these questions have located or stirred up in you a yearning for a simpler, more serene lifestyle, then I invite you to journey with me toward a place called Simplicity. On the way, we will explore some inspiring philosophies for simple living and share the experiences of some ordinary folk who are in the process of discovering its liberating joys. We will also look at some practical ideas for simplifying your life in the areas of your time, your leisure, your home and money and work. You will even be invited to follow a Brass Tacks Simplicity Plan by which you can begin the deliberate process of charting a simpler course for your own life.

But this is not a book of rigid rules on the way things *should* or *ought* to be done. (I'm on this journey, too, and I definitely don't have all the answers yet!) It does not seek to scold you for the complications in your life or place blame for the terrible situation the world is in today. It won't try to cram you into someone else's stripped-down lifestyle or push you into a drastic, traumatic change. Instead, it offers resources of encouragement and hope, gently pointing you toward solutions that fit your priorities and apply to your special circumstances. It offers a variety of suggestions on how to begin simplifying things one simple way at a time.

Never mind if you've tried to simplify before and you've ended up right back in the same old tangle of confusion. What is impossible in our own strength is entirely possible in God's power! If the quiet beauty of simple living sounds appealing to you, you can trust him to begin carving a road that leads through your complicated circumstances, whatever they are, to a place called Simplicity.

So what are we waiting for? Let's begin!

1

A Step Toward Simplicity

*A*nd after long years of spiritual homelessness, of nostalgia, here is that mystic loveliness of childhood again. Here is home. An old thread, long tangled, comes straight again.

—Marjorie Kinnan Rawlings

❧

I think I've always believed in the existence of a place called Simplicity—a place where people can slow down and unravel the complications of their lives. I've spent vacations there and a few wonderful spiritual retreats. I just never thought it was possible to live there full time.

And then, one year and one month ago, a small moving van chocked to the gills with our belongings took an important turn off of Interstate 10 and headed east. Down one rural highway, then another, it followed close behind us, down a winding blacktop that dwindled into a bumpy red-clay lane to the fourth telephone pole on the left, where we turned down the sandy trail that would lead us to our new home. This is the place we call Juniper Landing, a tiny, picturesque log cabin surrounded by acres of pines and oaks and juniper trees, sitting high on the bluff of a deep, cool Alabama river. After eleven years of coming here on weekends and vacations, after eleven years of talking about the "someday" when we just might move out here to stay, here we finally were . . . just Spike and me.

A True Confession

I might as well confess to you right up front that I'm married to a man named Spike. You would have found it out eventually anyway. It's not that he doesn't have a real name. It's Robert. But when he was an innocent baby, unable to defend himself, his Uncle Bubba nicknamed him "Spike." If your name was Uncle Bubba, you'd probably want to take it out on someone, too!

Spike and I have known each other since we were children. (He likes to say we had adjoining cribs, but that is a bit of an exaggeration.) At first glance it might seem that the two of us have little in common. By nature, Spike is easygoing. I'm ambitious. He orders a few needed items now and then from catalogs. I have a black belt in militant shopping. He studies birds and photographs wildflowers and communes with nature. I go to lunch.

Spike is also what you might call a true outdoorsman. I, on the other hand, have spent much of my life treating the out-of-doors like "something you walk through to get from the house to the car."[1]

We actually do share many things, however. We adore each other and our children, to begin with. We both love music and books and travel. We have the same crazy sense of humor. And we both love the Lord, which affects our opinions about everything else.

But probably the quickest agreement Spike and I ever came to on any subject was the day we first laid eyes on this beautiful, tranquil spot on the river that we now call home. It was love at first sight for both of us. However, I didn't know at the time that what he saw in his

A Step Toward Simplicity

mind's eye when he looked at this place was something quite different from what I saw.

I saw a retreat where we could come now and then to untangle our busy lives and rest and be refueled to go back into our normal rat race. I saw a vacation getaway. But I believe Spike always saw a home. In the back of his mind, I think he could always see the day that the moving van would be pulling up to the cabin and unloading the stuff of our lives to stay.

A Sense of Unreality

Looking back to the actual day of that move, I realize now how "out of it" I was. Have you ever felt so detached from a situation that it almost seemed as though you were hovering just above it, watching it happen to someone else? That's exactly how I felt as I stood watching the movers take our things out of the van. I remember thinking that I should be feeling excited, or maybe apprehensive or jubilant . . . or at least *something*. But all I really felt was numb. And tired.

We had just driven away from our roomy, suburban home an hour away in Mobile—the home where we had lived for the past nineteen years and raised our two sons. We had just driven away from everything that felt familiar and predictable and comfortable. In just a matter of hours, the movers had packed us up lock, stock, and lifestyle and transported us far away from the safe and predictable places and people I loved. This new life we were embarking on would bring enormous change for both of us—but especially for me.

I tried to remind myself of all the reasons we had decided to make this move. To begin with, our "nest," which only recently had seemed to be bursting at the seams with the belongings and activities of our teenage sons and their friends, was suddenly empty. Curt, our oldest, had graduated from college and was studying the

A Step Toward Simplicity

Bible in Montana. Andy, our youngest, was living in an apartment, engaged to be married, working part time, and going to college. Our four-bedroom house seemed strangely quiet.

Moving to the country also seemed to make sense for us financially. Spike's work as a landman in the oil industry, which had buttered our bread very well for twenty-five years, had slowed down considerably during the oil slump of the late 1980s and had never really regained its momentum. We simply didn't need the expense of two houses.

But there had to be more to it than that. Why was I here really? Had I merely followed my husband out here to realize his dream of a simpler life? I try to be a pretty good wife, but I'm just not that self-sacrificing. There had to be a reason—my own reason—why I had agreed to leave my familiar, busy life in a city of three hundred and fifty thousand people for a log cabin in the "suburbs" of a community of three hundred and fifty.

In the weeks and months that followed our move, as I began the process of adjusting to the pluses and minuses of my new life, I asked myself that question many times. And little by little it has come to me. Little by little, my memory has unfolded scenes that have laid bare places in me I haven't visited in years. Little by little, reflection has revealed to me some answers.

I see now that I am more than just a supporting character in Spike's wilderness drama. This quest for simplicity is my story, too. This is something I have yearned for from a distance—perhaps a little unrealistically, but quite earnestly—for many years.

Perhaps you too have had a deep but distant yearning for a simpler life. Perhaps you can even remember some simpler time in your childhood that pulls you back.

For me, that memory is of a little place called Fishville.

A Memory of Fishville

In the summers of my early childhood, Simplicity was a town called Fishville—a rural community in the Louisiana piney woods where my cousin Sidney owned a rustic but wonderful cottage on a creek. Basically one room surrounded on all sides by screened porches, the cottage was appropriately dubbed The Wind Blows Inn. It was the place where we would go to meet our North Louisiana relatives for warm-weather fun and food and family time.

But Fishville was always more an attitude than an agenda. Crammed into the car with inner tubes and suitcases and sacks of groceries, my parents and siblings and I would start to think in the Fishville idiom as we made the two-hour trip from our home in Lafayette. As the car wound its way up from the muggy lowlands of Cajun Country into the thick green woods north of Alexandria, we even imagined we could feel the air growing cooler.

Our days in Fishville were remarkably the same. After breakfast we kids would splash in the creek, creating "playhouses" in the spindly roots of trees that lined its banks or building dams to create little "floating pools" or staging water-bug races. Later, after the adults were breakfasted and coffeed, we could usually persuade one of them to take us for a real "deep water" swim down at Cassan's Branch or up at Dean's Hole.

Meals there were memorable. My grandmother, "Mimi," her gray curls pressed damply to her forehead and the inevitable crystal drop of perspiration clinging to the tip of her nose, would coax culinary delights from an ancient green-enamel stove: fried chicken stacked on green Depression glass platters, bowls of sliced fresh tomatoes, corn on the cob, and jambalaya, Mimi's specialty. After lunch everybody, regardless of age, napped while whirring fans stirred the summer air and the various-pitched snores of assorted uncles harmonized in a gentle, reassuring lullaby. Then, in the afternoon, we might have another swim or play checkers or walk up to The Store. (The Store was owned and operated by Mr. Ed Hawthorn, who was also the mayor of Fishville and had once been honored on *The Ed Sullivan Show* as "The Laziest Mayor in the United States.")

Nobody was ever in a hurry to make things happen in Fishville. Days came and went in their own sweet time. Early evenings at the cottage, adults sat around in rockers, talking and laughing together, and scooping up whatever passing child seemed to need a lap to settle on. Neighbors from other summer houses sometimes happened by, often walking barefoot down the creek, which served as a central thoroughfare of sorts to the houses on its banks.

An Underground Stream

If I had to design a simple world, I'd be hard pressed to find a better model than Fishville, with its lazy, easy summer days and nights. I felt safe there, and happy, and good about my world. I understood the rules (which were few) and I knew I was loved (which was everything). So I think that for years I blended my ideas of simplicity along with my memories of Fishville into the same sweet nostalgia soup.

What are your memories of simplicity? What emotions do they stir up in you? Does simplicity seem like an unattainable fantasy or like a present-day possibility?

I confess that I have difficulty thinking of simplicity in the present tense. I've tended to look on it as something from another era, something confined to the screen porches and summer houses and gardens of another generation—or at very best as a serene place where one could briefly escape before returning to the real world. It has seemed at times like an unreachable rose of childhood, a beautiful idea that has been choked and overgrown by the practical, inevitable weeds of adult worry and work.

For the truth is that most of my adult life has been a carnival of people and appointments and commitments and responsibilities. It has been a juggling act in which I heroically kept dozens of different balls in the air: my husband and his agenda, my children and their agendas, my work and its agenda, not to mention myself and mine. My world has moved to an erratic rhythm—like a nonstop calliope with the hiccups—propelled by my strange, haphazard blend of absentmindedness and perfectionism. And it has often seemed that the many things I wanted to do and had to do and felt I should do were constantly colliding like bumper cars.

But lest you think all that confusion made me miserable, let me hasten to add that I have been pretty content with my bumper-car existence. The fact is, there is a part of me that thrives on confusion. Oh, I might complain noisily, but on some level I think I've really enjoyed cooking the casserole, typing the term paper, and bouncing the baby all at the same time. It makes me feel like I'm getting something done.

Psychologist Archibald Hart suggests that we folks who thrive on chaos may have actually gotten addicted to our own adrenaline, and when things get too tranquil we need a shot of chaos just to get the blood pumping.[2] Maybe he's right. I do get a kind of rush from heading off catastrophe just at the last moment.

And yet always, there was that other side of me. Always just beneath the surface of my crowded, busy, adrenaline-addicted days was a quiet memory of warm evenings and soft, slow conversation that echoed in me like the clear music of a summer creek. Always a quiet kind of yearning ran just beneath my conscious chaos like an underground stream beneath a busy city street.

A Step Toward Simplicity

Simplicity Heroes

Most of the time, this underground yearning for simplicity came out in the books I loved and the people I admired. As a child, I loved the story of Wendy who made a home in a tree, no less, for Peter and the Lost Boys. I loved *The Swiss Family Robinson*, in which a shipwrecked family created a lovely life apart from civilization. I loved Little Dorritt, the Charles Dickens character whose simple honesty and resourcefulness shone in contrast to the spoiled pretensions of the British aristocracy.

Later, as I matured, my heroes were always the strong, balanced women in books and movies and real life who possessed the inner resources to carve out a simple but gracious life from their surroundings, however limited or hostile. Like Marjorie Kinnan Rawlings, who moved her typewriter and her stubborn sense of style into the backwoods culture of rural Florida and lived out her life there, writing bestsellers like *Cross Creek* and *The Yearling*. Or like Jean Paget, the heroine of Nevil Shute's *A Town Like Alice*, whose wit and courage helped her not only to survive as a World War II prisoner in Malaya, but later to make a life in the dusty and desolate outback of Australia as the wife of her wartime love, Joe Harmon.

I loved Helene Hamph in *84 Charing Cross Road*, who filled her tiny, thrifty New York apartment with treasured old volumes of literature she bought for next to nothing through the mail from a secondhand book shop in London. Most of all, I loved the simple old Dutchwoman, Corrie ten Boom, who lived much of her old age out of a suitcase, traveling throughout all the continents of the world to spread the Good News of the Lord who had brought her through the nightmare of the Nazi death camps.

But I must admit I was probably influenced by one

real-life "simplicity hero" more than any other. A hero who staunchly sought simplicity as the Holy Grail, who quietly but stubbornly traveled his own simple road, regardless of others around him. A hero who persisted in the belief that simplicity is a reality and the simple life is a possibility well within the grasp of those who are willing to reach for it.

That hero, of course, is Spike.

I'm touched each time I realize how patiently this lovely, low-key guy waited for me to change my strong but cluttered mind about moving to the country. He contented himself with camping trips and fishing trips and other part-time ventures into simplicity, living happily in the city with me until I was completely ready to launch out on this full-time adventure.

I smile now to remember all the summer evenings we'd sit out here on the front porch by the river, day-dreaming and wondering and idly talking about what it would be like to move here permanently. Out here, Spike could garden and do carpentry and woodcarving and maybe even take up painting again. Out here, without the distractions of living in town, perhaps I could actu-ally find time to write the novel I had always yearned to write. In this beautiful, tranquil environment, maybe I could even win the war against my migraine headaches. And, of course I always pictured friends and family driv-ing out for visits every weekend, for picnics and canoe rides and long, lazy conversations.

Easier Read Than Done

But our life here at Juniper Landing this past year has not been a perfect realization of all those fond day-dreams of the simple life. It has not been one long tran-quil traipse through our own personal South Alabama version of Eden. In the course of a year, all of the phi-losophy and poetry I had enjoyed on the subject of simplicity and all of the "how to" books I had read about creating a simpler lifestyle have been challenged. I have discovered that simplicity, like most worthwhile pursuits, is easier read than done.

There have been many times out here in the wilds of rural Alabama when I have found myself wondering if this dream of a "simpler life" is even possible—and if so, if it is worth it! There have been many mornings when I've asked myself what a nice civilized girl like me is doing in a place like this.

There was, for instance, the morning of the snake. Several weeks after the move, I was here all alone at the cabin getting a little light housekeeping done before tackling a writing assignment in my office. As I was absentmindedly carrying a basket of clean clothes in from our outdoor laundry area, not looking where I was going, I literally tripped over a huge, grayish, shiny reptile coiled by the back screen door. A SNAKE!!! Clothes flew in every direction as I literally threw down the basket and fled posthaste!

If I had been dressed, I probably would have jumped in the car and driven away, never to return! But alas, I was in my bathrobe, and my car keys were in the cabin. Cautiously I stood trembling at a respectful distance, staring at his dreaded, shiny self curled up there on my porch like my worst nightmare.

I waited. He didn't seem to be moving a scale. He didn't seem to be in much of a hurry. Surely, I thought, he's got things to do. Surely he'll just snake off in a minute or two and get on with the rest of his life. But he just sat there. Or lay there.

All kinds of thoughts crossed my mind. Maybe I had stunned him when I tripped over him and he was in some kind of a snake coma. Maybe he was really ticked off and was waiting there for me to come back so he could get revenge. Minutes passed—ten, fifteen, twenty.

This is ridiculous! I thought. *I don't have time for this snake. I've got to put this laundry away and finish rewriting my chapter by this afternoon.*

Carefully, gingerly, I gathered first one piece of laundry and then another, tiptoeing, moving slowly, gradually drawing closer and closer to my reptilian intruder. As I drew nearer, I noticed that his head had slithered between the slats in the floor of the back porch and that he was gradually inching out of the picture. I figured he had decided to let bygones be bygones. So this time, just as calm as you please, I stepped over my scaly guest, opened the screen door just wide enough to slip through it without disturbing him any further, and got back to business as usual. But all day long I kept saying to myself a little incredulously, "A snake! I stepped over a snake this morning!"

The Complications of Simplicity

I'm really thankful now that "Mr. No-Hips" (Spike's nickname for snakes) showed up that day so soon after the move. In a way it was a symbol of the challenges I'd be facing. And my decision to step over him was symbolic, too.

But my biggest challenge at Juniper Landing has not been snakes. My biggest challenge has been missing all the friends I was so used to seeing during the week. I've spent a ton of money on long-distance calls. I've also spent more time in traffic than I ever did in town, driving back and forth to Mobile for visits—a fact that has complicated my simplicity considerably.

A few of the other petty irritations that have complicated my new life have been a lack of storage space, tiny (almost nonexistent) closets, sand in everything, no dishwasher, yellow flies in the summer, and well water that makes my hair gooey. Our tiny house, which seemed roomy enough for weekends, has felt confining and close on a full-time basis.

Perhaps you have discovered your own set of irritations and complications in your quest for simplicity. If you haven't, you probably will. As near as I can tell, most people on this journey have discovered that simplicity is a concept that is anything but simple to grasp and a lifestyle that is anything but simple to attain. But nothing worth having is attained without some kind of struggle. Richard Foster writes in *The Freedom of Simplicity* that "seldom in life is there any issue of significance that will yield to easy answers."[3] Simplicity is certainly no exception to that rule—at least, not in my experience.

So this has been a year of wrestling with the ambiguities and the complications in my life that have kept simplicity at bay. It has been a year of pinpointing the million unnecessary ways I have allowed my life to be so complicated and of evaluating the faulty motives and petty payoffs that have kept me bogged down in confusion. This year I have had to let go of some beliefs that tend to perpetuate chaos and claim some others that bring about serenity. It has been a year of seeking, asking, knocking . . . and making a few compromises.

A Fishville Attitude

And what life-changing truths have I learned through all of this wrestling? Perhaps the most important is that Simplicity, like Fishville, is more of an attitude than an agenda.

We're definitely not involved in a Fishville agenda out here. We're not on vacation. I've probably put in more hours at my word processor in the year I've lived here than I had put in since I began writing. And Spike, when he's not working as a landman, has been doing the backbreaking job of remodeling our cabin.

But though we don't have a Fishville agenda, many days we do have a Fishville attitude. Though we're working harder, somehow we're not pushing as hard. We are more focused, because there are fewer distractions. We've become more intentional about taking time off, about giving ourselves permission to enjoy being human beings rather than "human doings." We're enjoying each other and our surroundings. And we're finding more opportunities to let our heavenly Parent scoop us up into his lap and love us just as we are. Living out here in our simple surroundings really has helped us simplify our attitudes as well.

But that raises a question: Do you have to live by a river to have a Fishville attitude? I am convinced the answer is no. In fact, it has become very clear to me during this life-changing year that simplicity is not necessarily linked to location. Moving into a log cabin won't suddenly make you simple, any more than moving into a college dorm will suddenly make you educated. Depending on the kind of person you are, depending on your specific calling and direction, your life might actually be complicated by a move to a rural setting like ours.

I have gradually realized that the simplicity we are finding here is less linked to our setting than to our direction—our spiritual commitment to live more simply, our determination to make simplifying choices, and our willingness to clarify and stand by certain goals and priorities.

Inner beliefs and commitments always have far more power to change our lives than any external move we can make. That is why I feel confident saying that if you really desire simplicity, if you are sincerely seeking, asking, and knocking, then the door to a simpler life will open to you. And this will be true whether you live in a city apartment, a small-town neighborhood, a suburban setting, or a cabin in the woods. In fact, to a greater degree than most of us realize, simplicity lies within our grasp wherever we are, if we are willing to go after it wholeheartedly.

The great writer and naturalist Henry David Thoreau believed that the seeker after a simpler life could find it best by advancing steadily toward it one small choice at a time. He wrote that as a person gradually "simplifies his life, [even] the laws of the universe will appear less complex."[4] As we move toward spiritual simplicity in the small choices of our lives, everything begins to seem simpler. As the avenues of our minds and spirits are cleared, even the cosmic issues of life seem to simplify.

Simplicity can begin for you as it did for me—as nothing more than an underground yearning, a prayer of the heart. This yearning can become a belief that becomes an attitude or a mindset that leads to a series of small choices that impel a series of small changes in the way we do things. And it is these small changes that finally (if diligently clung to) can begin to become a lifestyle.

Your Own Journey

I do not know you. I do not know your life or your circumstances or the elements of your existence that crowd out your peace. You may be longing to be liberated from overscheduled days and overextended finances. You may be yearning to cut through some of the sophistication and moral pollution of today's leisure activities and rediscover the joy of simple pleasures. Or perhaps you've lost a simple faith somewhere in the overgrowth of convoluted theories and dead-end doubts that abound in our culture, and you'd like to reclaim it.

There is so much I want to share with you—ideas and insights that have changed my life and that I hope can open you up to a new ease and clarity and inner serenity. If you were here, we might sit out on our screen porch this evening and talk it over while the breeze blows off the river, while the night sounds of whippoorwills and frogs and crickets make background music and the moon rises and reflects in the water. If you like to read in bed, you could crawl up in our big four poster and stay up as late as you like reading this book. Then you could sleep in tomorrow, because that's allowed here.

But it doesn't really matter where you are when you discover these ideas. I believe you will discover them. For yourself. Just by nature of the fact that you are reading this book, I believe you are already on your own journey to your very own place called Simplicity.

A Step Toward Simplicity

2

Homesick for Eden

I want a singleness of eye, a purity of intention, a central core to my life... to live "in grace" as much of the time as possible.... By grace I mean an inner harmony, essentially spiritual, which can be translated into outward harmony.

—Anne Morrow Lindbergh

One of the most unsettling things I do every day is watch the evening news. Thirty minutes worth of little thumbnail sketches about what's new on planet Earth can sometimes leave me feeling I've been tuned in to a Salvador Dali painting.

Last night it really got to me. Right after Peter Jennings said his fond farewells, I turned off the set and walked out into the fading summer afternoon, into the bright tangle of blooms in our garden, and thought about what I had just seen—the sad, sordid, tragic little bag of events I had just been made party to.

There was a story about a group of Satan-worshiping teens accused of ritually murdering some other kids in their neighborhood in a small heartland community. There was a report about the rise of AIDS among heterosexuals. There was a cute, old couple in Colorado who had lost their life savings and their home in some sort of bond swindle. There was a Supreme Court ruling that granted a religious sect in Florida the right to continue sacrificing goats and chickens as part of their religious worship service.

And then, of course, there was the nightly war story—this one about Bosnians killing Serbs and Serbs killing Bosnians and both groups of them weary and starving from the ongoing battle, but neither willing to call it quits. (That story closed with a heart-wrenching close-up of a little Bosnian girl's dirty, tearstained face, an image that still haunts me as I am writing this.)

Even the lighthearted human-interest tidbit they threw out at the end of the hour just to perk me up didn't help much. It was about a Japanese motorcycle club whose members dress up like California highway patrol officers and ride American-made Harley Davidson bikes all over Japan.

It's a pretty wacky world out there, folks. If you don't believe me, tune in tonight at 5:30 Central!

The Original Plan

Sometimes after one of my bouts with the evening news, I find myself thinking, "Surely things were never meant to be like this."

They weren't, you know. In fact, I believe that one of the main reasons for our deep dissatisfaction with all the confusion in our lives is that something inside tells us we were designed for something very different—something simple and sensible and lovely and right. We were designed to walk through a green garden with a good God, communing intimately with him in the cool of the day, trusting in his provision, marveling at his creation, and enjoying his friendship forever.

That was the original plan. That was where it all began.

But the tranquillity of that green garden was rather short lived. From the moment that our spiritual forebears sampled the fruit of a certain tree, things began to get complicated here on planet Earth. Two people who had needed nothing but air and praise and sunshine suddenly needed things like clothes and a place to hide.

But that's such an old, old story, you're probably thinking. *Why bring it up now? What does it have to do with our modern brand of chaos and unrest?*

Everything, it seems to me. In fact, the more I think about it, the more convinced I am that my own deep, underground yearning for simplicity harkens back to a much earlier time than my Fishville days. I really believe that in me—in all of us—is an almost genetic awareness that we were created for a simpler life than the one we know. That is what makes us sad sometimes in a way we can't quite explain. We are homesick for the simplicity of the original plan.

It was that inner longing for a lost quality of life that I struggled to express in my lyric, *Homesick For Eden*:

> The garden was green, the water was
>   clean,
> The animals came without names,
> And love was a girl who walked through
>   a world
> Where passion was pure as a flame.
> In the back of our minds is a time before
>   time
> And a sad, irreversible fact:
> We can't seem to think why we left there,
> And we can't seem to find our way back.
>
> For all of us are homesick for Eden,
> We yearn to return to a place we've never
>   known.
> Deep is the need to go back to the
>   Garden,

A yearning so strong for a place we
belong,
The place that we know is home.[1]

A Shimmering Quality

Do you remember your first experience with homesickness? I felt it for the first time when I was only seven years old. I had never been away from my parents for more than a night when I arrived at Camp Windywood for a three-week stay. The camp was beautiful, the people were kind, and I was learning to do wonderful things like ride horses and paddle canoes. I had every reason to be happy there . . . but one. There was an ache at the center of me like a great wound. It stayed with me all day long. And at night, after lights-out in the cabin, I could see my mama's face and feel my daddy's arms, and I would cry into my pillow until I fell asleep.

Just thinking about Eden sometimes gives me that same ache in my chest. I find myself wondering about the pure and shimmering quality of life there that somehow slipped through our fingers.

Just picture it. It was nothing to begin with. Nothing. And then God opened his mouth and spoke, and when he did, *everything* started taking shape. He used his words to make a world! He called forth forces of symmetry and beauty and great power. He laid boundaries of order and balance and proportion. With the precision of a master clockmaker he set in motion the weights and wheels of a perfect creation. And then, seeing the beauty of his own handiwork, he proclaimed with pride, "Good. Good." And "Very good."

Light, darkness, sky, land, water, winds, and tides; plants, trees, sun, moon, stars, and planets—all these he made and celebrated. And creatures—flying, soaring, swimming, loping, crawling, galloping. All things in their vast array he created.

Then finally he created human beings, both male and female—his shining glory, whom he put in charge of it all.

A Simple Life

Life for the man and the woman in Eden was beautiful and simple and complete. They had an inner sense of connectedness to the rhythm of the world around them. They were all of a piece with God and his creation.

There was no ambiguity about who was in control there. Adam and Eve knew that God was God and they were not. They understood the rules, too, because there was only one: Do not eat the fruit of a certain tree. So what was sanctioned was bountiful. What was forbidden was spelled out in no uncertain terms. And within those clear and simple boundaries, those two people were free to walk through the glory of each passing day, enjoying God and each other and their beautiful new home.

Maybe you're thinking what I'm thinking just about now. How in creation could a place as simple and lovely as Eden have turned into the crazy, chaotic world I saw on the news last night?

At the risk of gross oversimplification, I'd summarize it by saying that Adam and Eve listened to the wrong voice and made the wrong choice. It was plain "garden variety" temptation, not very different from what we know today, that wrecked the Garden.

The Incident of the "Bloodsuckers"

It was not all that different, come to think of it, from a time when our youngest son, Andy, listened to the wrong voice, made the wrong choice, and wrecked our next-door neighbor's garden. (The stakes were higher in Adam and Eve's situation, I'll grant you. But temptation is temptation!)

It happened shortly after we moved to Mobile. Little Andy, a preschooler at the time, ran out to play, hoping he could tag along with his big brother, Curt, and Curt's new friends, Danny and David. When the older boys realized how eager Andy was to be part of the crowd, they must have seen him as an easy target for peer pressure. I'm still not sure which one of the older boys came up with the idea, but they decided to talk Andy into doing a little neighborhood vandalism.

Our new next-door neighbors, Mr. and Mrs. Temple, were an older couple who spent most of their retirement hours cultivating their yard. It was magnificent—beautiful enough to be in any magazine. They had just put out almost a truckload of lush green and red caladiums in their front-yard beds. They were a shoo-in for "Yard of the Month."

"You see those big, green plants with the red spots in the middle?" one of the older boys said to Andy, pointing at the Temples' caladiums. Andy nodded enthusiastically. "Those are bloodsuckers," he told him, "And if you don't pull up every one of them, they are going to take over the whole neighborhood. Go get 'em!"

"I can't," Andy protested. "I'll get in trouble."

"No way," the older boys assured him. "Your mom won't care. In fact, she'll be glad."

Andy hesitated in the grip of temptation. He had always been one of those children who delighted in a little chaos. He sorely wanted to play with those big boys. And never before had he been handed such a persuasive rationalization for doing something that sounded like so much fun.

"Aw, come on," the others coaxed.

With a wild look in his eye, Andy charged into the immaculate, manicured yard next door. Wildly and enthusiastically, he began pulling up the "bloodsuckers" by their roots as poor Mrs. Temple looked out of her window aghast.

Later he tried to explain that he only did it to save the neighborhood. He also mentioned that the other

Homesick for Eden

boys had put him up to it. But none of these rationalizations seemed to impress the adults in the situation. Just as he had feared in the first place, Andy was in trouble!

Clues to Confusion

Adam and Eve's disobedience had somewhat broader repercussions than Andy's assault on the "bloodsuckers." When our first ancestors took a bite of the forbidden fruit, they lost far more than just a beautiful landscape. What they had done was to shred the seamless garment of life as they had known it. What had been simple was no longer simple. Gone was their feeling of connectedness, their clear sense of identity, their understandable boundaries, and their primary trust relationships.

An understanding of these losses is important to us today, because they are still affecting our lives. Each one provides a clue to why our modern world is so deeply mired in chaos and confusion.

The Loss of Connectedness

Ever since Eden's doors were shut, people have known what it is to feel "cut off" and disconnected. Feelings of alienation and estrangement are common causes for stress. Even the most loved, nurtured, and well rounded of us has probably experienced some times of feeling "out there all alone," separated from God and others.

I remember how touched I was the first time that our little son, Curt, who was only eight at the time, shared his lonely, "cut off" feelings with me. It was a rainy day, and we were riding in the car together, silently listening to the rhythmic swishing of the windshield wipers. I could tell he was gearing up for a real "heart to heart."

"Mama," he finally said, "When you hear sad music, do you ever just want to run into the night and cry?"

"Yes," I answered, very surprised at his earnestness. "I do." The windshield wipers took over for a minute as I thought about his question. "I'll tell you one song that makes me feel that way. It's Paul Simon's song, 'America'—you know, the part where it says, 'I'm empty and aching and I don't know why.'"

"Oh, Mom," Curt blurted out, "that's just how I feel sometimes. I feel empty and aching and I don't know why." Then he paused and thought about it. "Where does Paul Simon live anyway?" he asked. "And how does he know what it feels like to be a little boy in Mobile, Alabama?"

How could Paul Simon's beautiful description of his own feelings so deeply move a little boy in a different part of the country hundreds of miles away? I think it is because the lonely feelings he described are universal to all of us. I have come to think of these empty, cut-off feelings as "fallout from the Fall."

Tom Wingo, the hero of Pat Conroy's novel, *The Prince of Tides*, was a character who was haunted by feelings of alienation all of his adult life. He expressed them like this:

> I fear emptiness in life, vacuity, boredom, and the hopelessness of a life bereft of action. It is the death-in-life . . . that sends a primeval shiver through the nerves and open pores of my soul. If I catch a fish before the sun rises, I have connected myself again to the deep hum of the planet. If I turn on the television because I cannot stand an evening alone with myself or my family, I am admitting my citizenship with the living dead.[2]

Many of us, like Conroy's hero, feel a deep unconscious yearning to be reconnected to the gentle pulse of this planet. And I believe that yearning we feel is really a homesickness in our spirits for a Garden we've never even seen with our human eyes.

The Loss of Identity

Adam and Eve lost something else when they transgressed the boundaries of Eden. They lost the clear, simple sense of their own identity. That picture of themselves that they had found reflected in the loving eyes of the One who designed them was blurred and distorted when they rebelled against him. Suddenly they were ashamed of the bodies they had felt so good about. Suddenly they were scrambling for fig leaves and a good hideout.

Many of us carry in us the destructive payoff for Eden's wrong choice. We find our image in the eyes of imperfect others (parents, peers, teachers, etc.) and develop a faulty sense of self.

There was a beautiful young woman named Tana in my freshman class at LSU. Tana was an art major and very talented. She was also as delicate and lovely as a Dresden doll, with huge, clear blue eyes and hair like pale-yellow silk. I always admired her and thought of her as someone who had everything.

Years after we left college, Tana and I became close friends. I'll never forget how stunned I was when she confided to me that all during her college years she had been painfully insecure about her looks and her self-worth. Tana had no idea how beautiful or special she was. And even when I tried to tell her how much I had always admired her, I could tell she had a hard time believing or accepting my sincere compliment.

An unhealthy and unrealistic sense of self can make our lives miserable and even ruin our health. I have known more than one anorexic teen who has stubbornly tried to starve herself because she saw her thin body as fat. I have another gorgeous friend who has won major beauty competitions, yet she sees her flaws far more clearly than she sees her strong points.

My friend and Bible teacher, Pam, says she believes there is a little voice that lives in our mirrors and talks to our insecurities. It tries to convince us that we are ugly or fat or old or whatever it is that we most fear. (Personally, I believe it is the same "little voice" which spawned Eden's rebellion.) Pam has learned that when she spends her first hour in the morning "settling" her identity in God, she never hears that voice at all!

But our loss of identity often goes deeper than our looks. We try to acquire a feeling of significance in many other areas as well: our work, our achievements, our bank accounts, our social standing, our "connections." Adam and Eve in the Garden did not need any of these things to prove their value; they were able simply to be. But our chaotic culture has us running around in circles trying to find our worth in doing.

The year I worked in the advertising industry, I saw firsthand that fortunes are made and empires built on the shaky self-images of prospective consumers. Every ad I wrote was aimed at convincing buyers that purchasing this car or shopping at that store or dining at this restaurant would finally make them feel whole and happy and fulfilled—that with one simple purchase they would finally, magically possess the self-confidence they had been lacking.

But the truth is, no amount of money can buy back for us that true, balanced, sense of self-worth that was left behind in Eden. It can only be found where Adam and Eve found it, in the eyes of the One who made us.

The Loss of Boundaries

Another valuable thing that was lost when Eden shut its gates was a clear sense of boundaries. Adam and Eve had more or less been given *carte blanche* in their little kingdom. There was only one law on the books, and no one had broken it yet, so there was no confusion, no guilt, no shame. There were no gray areas for the courts to interpret. All the players understood the rules.

Not so in our complicated world today. Moral boundaries are constantly being stretched and pushed back. Ethical blacks and whites are so badly smudged that the lines are all but lost. Nobody is sure of the rules anymore.

So what do we do? A lot of the time, we make up our own rules.

I've noticed morality surveys lately in several women's magazines. Readers are invited to fill in forms that reveal what their beliefs and their moral boundaries are and to send the forms in to the magazine. The findings of these surveys are then published almost as a guideline for readers. It is as if the magazine morality graph is saying, "Here is what most people are doing. If your morality falls somewhere within the boundaries of what most people do, then you must be doing okay." The magazine morality graph reinforces my belief that people hunger for boundaries. They will even invent their own if they think none exist.

During my training to be a teacher, I discovered that the human need for rules and boundaries begins early in life. As part of our preparation for student teaching, we elementary education majors were required to spend hours observing children in the classroom and on the playground. One of the things I noted about children at play was that they'd almost always spend the first part of their playtime making up the rules. There was usually a lot of heated talk back and forth about what would be permitted and what would be "against the rules," and only after the boundaries were established would the game begin.

Life in our culture is like those playground games, in a way. Since almost anything goes these days when it comes to morality, people feel compelled to create their own morality graphs and ethics codes. My mom has noticed in her practice of psychology that children who grow up without being given moral boundaries become adults who have to cope with the daily stress of inventing their own morality. Looking back through the tangle of moral and ethical mazes our society now lives in, how simple Eden seems!

The Loss of a Simple Trust Relationship

Probably the heaviest consequence of what happened in Eden is that God's children got separated from him. Man and woman turned their backs on the central relationship of trust in their lives—a relationship which had been their anchor and their focus—and human beings have been lost ever since.

One of my favorite recent movies, *City Slickers*, has a funny scene that homes in on our need for that central focus. In this scene, character actor Jack Palance, who plays the road-worn trail boss, volunteers to tell the main character, played by Billy Crystal, "the secret of life." Here, in effect, is how the scene goes:

> "This," says the trail boss, holding up his index finger, "is the secret of life."

> Crystal looks confused. "Your finger is the secret of life?"

> "No," the trail boss explains. "One thing. That is the secret of life."

> "Okay, I give," shrugs Crystal. "What is the one thing?"

> "You'll have to figure that out for yourself" is the trail boss's enigmatic answer.

Though these lines got a pretty good laugh from the audience the night we saw the movie, I recognized the truth in the "trail boss philosophy." The fragmented quality of our lives today is often traceable to the loss of that "one thing," that central focus. We have lost our "unifying center." We are like planets gone wild, flying off in all directions, trying to revolve around too many suns. We were created to be centered in the one, true God, and without him we lack our essential center of gravity.

But we Americans are a very resourceful people. Whatever we lack, we simply invent, and everywhere today people are inventing their own gods. Money. Success. Ideas. Even ourselves. Certain New Age gurus assure us that we ourselves are gods. Well, this may be called a New Age idea, but it is, in fact, a temptation which is as old as the Garden. Deciding that we can be our own gods is deciding to have a food binge on forbidden fruit.

God invented us. It's not up to us to invent him— not in anybody's image, and especially not our own. He was and he is and he will be himself, whether we decide to "give him a break" and believe in him or not.

Our son Curt made this point pretty well in a senior editorial for his college paper:

> Jesus is not a myth, he is not a ghost, he is not a cosmic theophany. God came down from heaven and walked among us two thousand years ago in the form of a man, Jesus. People touched him; he ate fish and burped. ... Yes, he was real. This really happened. Jesus loved everybody, even the selfish, conceited, brokenhearted people who didn't understand him. It was for those people that he died.... The above truths are not true because I want them to be true or because I am able to recognize their truth. God was here a long time before I was, he's here in

this room with me right now . . . and he'll be here long after I complete my petty posturing and return to dust. I am his creation and it is immensely mind-blowing that I even exist at all.[3]

Missing Your Dad

Last night standing in my little garden after the evening news was not the first time I've felt homesick for Eden. I have felt it many other times too. Sitting in a divorce court several years ago with a close friend who was facing the end of her marriage. Or caught in a snarl of rush-hour traffic with horns honking and angry faces behind every windshield. Or looking at an old picture of friends I've loved and shared my life with who have moved away.

At times like these, when I'm wondering why life has to be so fractured and so complicated, I find myself yearning for the serenity of that simple place where two people really knew who they were and where they stood. Where there was a sense of connectedness, understandable boundaries, and a primary trust relationship in the middle of it all.

Standing there last night in the midst of all of those swirling memories and feelings, I suddenly remembered something very important about homesickness. The child who is away isn't the only one who suffers. At home, most likely, the parents are feeling it, too.

I remembered so clearly the weekend we drove up through the Smoky Mountains to Sewanee, Tennessee, to leave Curt at college for his freshman year. That tremendous ache throbbed in my chest even as we were saying goodbye, and it hurt for weeks afterward. I missed my child, and I missed "the way it used to be" when we were tucking two little boys in bed at night. It would never be that way again.

And that is when it hit me that God is probably homesick for Eden, too. He's probably missing his children with a great ache in his loving Father heart. And he's probably missing the way it used to be before everything got so complicated between us and him.

And that is why he has not left us outside of Eden, looking wistfully through the locked gates, wishing we could get back in. He has built a bridge from our chaos back to his simplicity.

The bridge is not new. It is not the Creator's "Plan B." It is built of the love that he intended for us all along —the love that was there before the first foundations of heaven, before the day was split from the darkness.

This love was unfolded as light. This love was poured out as water. This love flowed forth as the rhythm of the Universe moving through the mind and the muscle and the miracle of all creation. This love was the Word that was there from the beginning. "Through him all things were made; without him nothing was made that has been made. In him was life, and that life was the light of men" (John 1:3).

Jesus is the central focus that reveals our hearts' priorities. He is the field of gravity that causes our far-flung affections to line up like planets around the center of his grace. He is the bridge that stretches across our chaotic circumstances and reconnects us with the simplicity of God's original plan for our lives.

Are you feeling a longing inside tonight for something you can't quite put your finger on? Do you understand tonight what Paul Simon meant when he wrote, "I'm empty and aching and I don't know why"?

Well, I think I know why. In the back of your mind, you're remembering a time before time, when things were simple and lovely and right. You're homesick— that's all it is. You're missing your Dad. And he's missing you, too.

Maybe you should call Home. Tonight.

43

3
Clearing the Cluttered Path

W

e have seen and known some people who seem to have found this deep Center of living where the fretful calls of life are integrated, where No as well as Yes can be said with confidence.

—Thomas Kelly

❦

If we were to strip our daily lives back to their simplest, most basic brain activity, that activity would be choosing. Choosing is the way we get from "here" to "there" on any given day.

Think about it. We choose to get out of bed or to pull the covers over our heads. We choose to eat breakfast or to skip it. We choose to eat healthy or to "pork it up." We choose to go to our jobs or to stay home and risk not having a job to go to. We choose to be concerned about others or to live totally for ourselves. And should we choose not to choose, even then we are choosing: In effect, we are choosing to let life choose for us!

Life-Changing Choices

I've never been very good at making even small choices. I get bogged down. I have been known to keep a long hairstyle I'm tired of, for example, just because I can't make up my mind how to get it cut. I'll spend excesses of time selecting a wallpaper pattern or an upholstery fabric. And I would warn you never to get behind me in a cafeteria line. Green beans or broccoli? Grilled shrimp or Salisbury steak? Finding myself faced with a whole row of choices, I quickly become paralyzed!

I remember a particularly difficult choice I had to make early in my songwriting career. I had just made contact with my first real, live music publisher, and (miracle of miracles!) this small company actually wanted to publish one of my songs. I was elated. I felt I had reached the pinnacle of success.

But Spike rightly perceived that this acceptance was just the tiniest baby step on a long uphill journey I would have to take if I really wanted to be a professional writer. He began to urge me to make a trip to Nashville in order to meet personally with these people who had taken an interest in my work.

If I had known then what I know now about the value of personal contact in the music industry, I wouldn't have had such a hard time deciding to make that first trip to Nashville. But from where I sat at the time, going there was a frightening prospect and a difficult choice. I realized it might be good to shake these people's hands in person and pull out some other songs for them to hear on the spot. But what if they hated my songs and I had to sit face-to-face with rejection? Writing songs in the comfortable security of my cozy little at-home office was one thing; forging out into an industry I knew nothing about was another.

In the end, I did choose to make the trip rather than stay cloistered in my own safe environment. My friend Betsy and I arrived in Nashville in the midst of what turned out to be one of the heaviest snowfalls that city had had in years. We ended up being stranded there for several days because Interstate 65 was closed.

That's the bad news. The good news was that choosing to take that initial step into the world of professional music was a life-changing decision. It was the beginning of a new career that has brought a new focus to my life. It has given me tremendous joy and allowed me to share my faith through my songs with many thousands of people over the past fourteen years.

For me, choosing to go to Nashville back in 1979 was a pretty dramatic example of how important our choices can be. But choosing to move toward a simpler life can have equally dramatic repercussions in our lives. Like my choice to go to Nashville, the choice for simplicity is one that moves us out of the familiar patterns of living into a place of growth. It can be a difficult decision, but it is an important, life-changing one.

The Summary of Our Choices

In a sense, of course, all our choices are life changing—even the little ones. If we were to unravel the fabric of our lives, I believe we would find that the very weave and pattern of who we are today has been largely determined by what we have chosen to do and say and be at each crossroad. Who we are is in some way a summary of lots of big and little choices.

Does that thought make you feel uncomfortable? It makes me squirm a little. I don't like to acknowledge that I have chosen my way into some of the jams I've found myself in. I feel more comfortable thinking of these choices as "reactions"; that way I don't have to take responsibility for them. But the truth is that our reactions are also choices, for we choose how we will react in each situation.

I learned this at an early age. Choosing was a big part of my upbringing. When Mom and Dad desired a certain kind of behavior from us kids, they would often

Clearing the Cluttered Path

put it to us in the form of a choice. For instance, Mom might say, "You have a choice. You can stop acting like a bunch of wild monkeys, or you can go to your room." If the wild-monkey behavior persisted, Mom would then say very sweetly (between clenched teeth), "I see you have *chosen* to go to your room!"

I never really intended to choose a state of exile in my room, but the result was the same. By choosing not to stop my wild-monkey behavior, I was , in effect, choosing my room.

Using this reasoning, you could say that Spike chose not to be a trumpet player by choosing to wrestle with Dinka deBoisblanc during band tryouts when we were in elementary school. He still thinks longingly of what a great jazz trumpeter he might be today if Dinka had not pushed him into the trash can just as it was his turn to try out. The exasperated band leader sent both Spike and Dinka back to their classrooms, and neither plays a band instrument to this day!

Directly or by default, we are choosing to live simple or complex lives every day. If your life is rushed or stressed or complicated, you may feel that circumstances or fate have somehow trapped you in your crazy lifestyle. But I would challenge you to look very closely at your life and see how often your choices are dictating the simplicity or the chaos in which you live. I really believe that when we are honest with ourselves we can see that, at least to some extent, we are choosing our way into the complicated conditions that confound us. At the very least, we are failing to choose a simpler way.

Too Many Options

In this three-ring circus of a culture, becoming adept "choosers" is fundamental to survival, because we are faced with an absurd number of choices on any given

Clearing the Cluttered Path

day—choices that range from mega to mundane.

Recently I was struck by what a plethora of choices we face as Americans when I read an account of a missionary returning to the United States from a Third World country. When queried about her greatest shock upon reentering this culture, she replied, "The potato chip aisle!" Having been out of the country for years, this young woman had not kept pace with all the kinds and colors and flavors and shapes of chips on the market, and she deeply resented the fact that so much energy had to be spent on such a trivial choice when there were so many more important things to decide.[1]

Most of us in this culture travel a road that is overgrown with options (important and trivial), and we won't get very far without developing some skills at choosing. Years ago I cut out a little slogan from the newspaper that said, "Failing to choose is choosing to fail." Our lives are never going to become simpler and more serene by accident.

Simplifying Choices

We will certainly never reach a place called Simplicity without learning to recognize and make *simplifying choices*—the kind of hard choices that make our lives simpler. How can we recognize a simplifying choice when one comes our way? I would suggest three simple clues:

❦ *A Simplifying Choice...*
Pares Down the Possibilities and
Weeds Out the Options

Most of us have already had some of our possibilities pared down and our options weeded out by what I call *circumstantial limitations*. Being born a girl, for instance, automatically limited my option to sing with a

Clearing the Cluttered Path

men's barbershop quartet. Being raised in Louisiana limited my option to learn snow skiing in my own backyard when I was growing up. Circumstantial limitations are those that are handed to us whether we like them or not. They can be physical, geographical, financial, or even cultural. We can overcome many of our circumstantial limitations, but we cannot avoid them.

But *voluntary limitations* are something quite different. The very word *voluntary* indicates that a choice has been involved. To limit our options voluntarily is to make a decision to do without something we could have had. It is choosing to curtail our own activities, to draw lines and set up boundaries where none have been required of us. Doing this can be a much more difficult prospect than merely learning to live with the limits over which we have no control.

One example of voluntarily limiting options might be choosing to live within a tighter budget in order to give more financial support to a shelter for the homeless. The easy and obvious thing would be to spend all of our money on our own needs and the needs of our families. But our compassion for homeless people might motivate us to voluntarily limit our spending and live more simply so that we can share what we have with them. Social scientist Duane Elgin emphasized the spiritual benefits of such choices when he said, "Voluntary simplicity is [choosing to live] more frugally on the material side of life so we can live more abundantly on the spiritual side of life."[2]

Jesus voluntarily limited his options. He was the all-powerful Son who was actually one with the Father. The book of John tells us that he was around from before the beginning of time and had a say in everything that was created. He was in what you might call a power position, with no limits or boundaries as we might think of them. Everything was a possibility for him. Yet one of the very

Clearing the Cluttered Path

first choices Jesus made regarding his existence on planet Earth was a choice to limit his options dramatically.

He could have arrived on lightning bolts, zapping whole cities with a single word. But instead, he arrived in one of the most fragile and vulnerable packages possible, the body of a newborn baby. He grew up in a family, learned a trade, and went to temple like other Jewish boys. When he began his ministry at the age of thirty, he traveled on foot, spoke to a few thousand people (often one at a time), discipled a handful of followers, and then died an inglorious death. But his "limited" human life had an unlimited impact on the whole world.

By choosing to limit his options, Jesus was able to show us the power and beauty of a simple life obediently lived. He was able to demonstrate all that a simple human vessel is capable of once it has been filled with the power of God. And when we follow his example and limit our options, our lives automatically become simpler. Even the smallest limitations can give us more room to breathe.

I learned this in a very practical way when we enrolled our two sons in a school that required them to wear uniforms. From day one, they hated the idea. Curt, especially, prided himself on being able to come up with original and sometimes outrageous outfits from his own motley mix of jeans and T-shirts, and he felt resentful that his "style" had been restricted and his options limited by this "preppy," school-prescribed wardrobe.

But being the mother in the scenario, responsible for supplying the clean clothes every day, I immediately appreciated the simplicity those uniforms brought into our lives. I was not having to scramble to launder anyone's favorite T-shirt at the last minute. There was no arguing or indecision about what would be worn. Every shirt was like every other. Every shirt matched every pair of slacks. Only one belt and one pair of shoes and one standard jacket was required. I was amazed at the amount of simple peace this one small limitation of options was able to bring into our lives on school mornings!

Artist Sue Bender learned the value of choosing to limit her options after living for a time among the Amish people. These "plain and simple" religious folk try hard to live as people did in less frantic times—before such modern inventions as electricity, automobiles, television, and credit cards. After experiencing their quieter, simpler way of life, Bender was able to recognize that her life in California had been a frantic chase in all directions, a chaotic venture driven by a gluttony for new and different experiences. She described it like this:

> My life was a crazy quilt, a pattern I hated. Hundreds of scattered, unrelated, stimulating fragments, each going off in its own direction, creating a lot of frantic energy. There was no overall structure to hold the pieces together.[3]

Among the Amish, Bender found a life as serene and orderly as the simple, geometric quilts made by the Amish women. She discovered that the "pieces" of their simple lives were fewer and were held together by a strong framework of beliefs, something her life had lacked.

After returning to California, Bender pared down some of the superfluous activity in her own life. As she did, she discovered that the things which remained were imbued with added significance simply by virtue of the fact that they were not crowded into such a hectic schedule. Paring down some of her possessions, activities, and relationships gave her a new ability to focus on the ones that remained.[4]

This idea of "focus" delivers us directly to the doorstep of the next clue to recognizing simplifying choices.

❦ A Simplifying Choice...
Focuses on the Foremost and Brings Passion to the Important

When I was a little girl, I was a doll fanatic. My room was crowded with what seemed to be limitless options where dolls were concerned. I had dolls of every size and kind, and I loved them all. But every Christmas, when I found that special new doll under the Christmas tree, I would put all of my other dolls away in the closet for a few weeks so that I could concentrate on "getting to know" and love my newest baby.

Though I didn't know at the time that I was following any kind of simplicity formula, I realize now that I was. I was giving myself room to focus on the foremost and bring more passion to the important.

So often we have the mistaken idea that the more things and activities and relationships we have in our lives, the more meaningful our lives will be. Ironically, the converse is often true. An overabundance of commitments and involvements actually tires us and drains the meaning out of even the richest experiences. Simply paring down the number of things that draw on our time and energy gives us a heightened excitement and a deepened caring for the select few that remain.

Spike has been using this principle as he landscapes the wooded land around our cabin. He selects the trees that are the most promising and beautiful and then takes down the little scrub trees around them that are competing with them for water and sunshine. The property still looks wooded and shady, but those select trees now stand out because of the clearing around them.

Focusing on the foremost in our lives works like that. As the peripheral activities and relationships are uprooted, we find that it's easier to devote our energies to the primary ones. When we find that some of our peripheral commitments are choking out our primary ones, for instance, we know it is time to take down some scrub oaks! With some of the nonessentials out of the way, the essentials have a chance to flourish. They become even more compelling and exciting to us.

Perhaps you already *know* that you are too busy doing too many things. Perhaps you already *know* that your peripheral commitments are choking your primary values. Perhaps you *know* that experiencing serenity and simplicity in your life depends on your choosing to weed out some of the nonessentials in order to focus on the essentials. But knowing and doing are two different things.

How do we actually begin paring down and weeding out so that we can focus with new passion on what matters? How do we know what does matter—which things should go and which should stay? Most of the activities we find ourselves involved in are worthy, enjoyable, necessary, or at least familiar. Most of the things we own were acquired with some purpose in mind, and we have at least some level of attachment to them. Most of the people we deal with are in our lives for a reason: We are related to them or in love with them or we work with them. We can't just begin throwing out things and activities and people without some kind of rationale—which brings us to the third clue to recognizing simplifying choices.

🐾 *A Simplifying Choice...*
Reflects a Positive Organizing Principle

Organization consultant Stephanie Winston contends that "all concepts of order...share one essential characteristic: an organizing principle...a central pole, an essential priority, around which all the other components group themselves." She contends that everything from clothes closets to rocket ships can be made more simple and orderly when their contents are grouped around this central idea.[5]

Look into anyone's closet, and you can immediately determine that person's essential priority or "organizing principle." My tiny closet's system of order is determined right now by my desperate need for space; all my storage decisions grow out of the need to cram my walk-in wardrobe into a cubbyhole closet. I have skirt trees and blouse hangers that can accompany four or five items of clothing. Sweaters are stacked five deep on the one available shelf along with plastic bins that accommodate running clothes, pantyhose, and scarves. Looking into the inner workings of my closet, I feel a bit claustrophobic. (This spring as we're remodeling, I'm more excited about getting a new closet than almost anything!)

My daughter-in-law, Jenni, went through a phase of organizing all of her separates by color. White blouses were hung together, print blouses were hung together, and so on. Her closet was a work of art.

I was amazed the first time I looked into my friend Nancy's closet. It is freshly papered, and the coat hangers aren't all jammed together like mine always are. Actually, they look so orderly that I suspect her of taking time to space them at neat, one-inch intervals. There are special compartments for different kinds of shoes, sweaters, scarves, belts, hatboxes, and many other items. Also, Nancy doesn't even hang up an item of clothing unless all the buttons are sewed on, the hem is taken up to the right length, and she knows she will look great in it when she puts it on! Order and beauty are the organizing principles for Nancy's closet.

When my son Andy was growing up, his closet was a completely different story. The organizing principle that governed his storage decisions was saving time for play; he wanted to spend as little time as possible on any organizational particulars. His essential priority was being with kids in the neighborhood or grabbing another snack or getting some extra sleep or anything but considering something as mundane as the state of his

Clearing the Cluttered Path

closet! You get the picture. Andy's closet was a full-time disaster area.

Our lives, like our closets, tend to be organized around an essential priority which motivates our choices. Each life revolves around its own central belief system, whether positive and true or destructive and faulty, clear and well thought out or muddled and haphazardly adopted. And each life will be shaped by choices that reflect that organizing principle, whether those choices are made consciously or unconsciously.

The few people I know whose lives revolve around a strong, sane, unifying organizing principle are delightful to be with, because they are so purely themselves. There is nothing fractured or split or the least bit confused about their personalities. What they do reflects what they believe and who they are. They truly are "uniquely unified."

I think, for example, of an elderly English missionary who stayed with us several times, once when he was eighty-eight years young. Norman's love for God and his Word was so deep and passionate that it had become his whole life. I remember being fascinated to see him "kick into gear" for sharing his experience of Christ in a teaching. He always seemed to drop fifteen or twenty years just by opening the Bible.

Another great example of a uniquely unified personality is my sister-in-law Valli. Her whole life has centered on her belief that she could make a difference in the lives of children. Unable to have children of their own, she and her husband, Brad, adopted a son, Daniel, and a daughter, Julie. During the preadoption process, Valli became aware of the many unadoptable children who need foster care until their own parents can care for them or their cases can be otherwise decided. Over the past seventeen years, Valli and Brad have welcomed dozens of foster children, many of them infants, into their home. Over the years, they have poured out their lives and love and resources for these children.

Valli would never have to think twice about her essential priority or organizing principle; she knows who she is and what she is called to be. Nor would she hesitate if asked to label the most valuable thing in the world. She would smile and tell you that it is a child.

The centered lives of people like Valli and Norman shine with simplicity. The strong, positive organizing principle in each of their lives has become a well from which strong, positive decisions are drawn.

Finding our own inner point of order, our own organizing principle, is a vital step toward simplicity, for whatever we put at the center of our personal solar system is destined in some sense to become the reigning factor in our lives. If we do not consciously adopt a positive, unifying organizing principle for ourselves, a negative one will all too gladly take the center spot.

A decade and a half ago, my calendar was literally jammed with activities, commitments, and responsibilities. I was busy every waking hour with club work, college classes, amateur theater, dance and exercise classes, and community service.

If you had asked me what my central priority was during this time, I would probably have tried to convince you that it was "my family." But with such a profusion of activities, it was difficult to tell what I really valued. I was constantly shuffling my children back and forth to different sitters, rushing in and out, giving them quick kisses, but not giving them enough quality time or attention.

Looking back at that time in my life, I see now that my unconscious organizing principle was my desperate need to please and to receive affirmation from others outside of my family. My inner point of focus was "people pleasing."

With such a scattered and fragmented life, no wonder I was soon facing a crisis in my marriage. Spike and I had begun to run on parallel tracks. We were in two different worlds emotionally. That was a difficult and painful time for me, but in the end it was a very positive one. It helped me begin to see what really mattered, and it helped me let go of what didn't.

Suddenly I knew I needed God in a serious way. I needed an unshakable central priority for my life to revolve around. I needed his unconditional love, which would quench my thirst for approval and affirmation. With God at the center, I found myself able to say "no" for the first time to the unnecessary extras. I began to find a real direction for my life.

Isn't it amazing how simple things become when something we treasure is threatened? Suddenly our priorities become crystal clear!

When a child is ill or a close friend dies or an all-important relationship is in trouble, there are no gray areas anymore. It suddenly becomes easy to see what is primary and what is merely peripheral. But what a shame that we must wait for a crisis to get our priorities in order. Our lives would be so much easier if we would take the time to look closely at our lives and begin focusing on the important things before a crisis comes.

As I began to reevaluate all of my time commitments that year in the light of my faltering marriage, I began to make some simplifying choices. With Christ as my "strong center," my life became simpler, and my marriage began to recover. The serenity of that season in my life was a new experience.

Step by Step to Simplicity

But even though my life became simpler that year than ever before, I soon learned that simplicity is not a one-time decision. I have to keep choosing it one day at a time. Every choice I make today will take me a little closer or a little farther away from that place called Simplicity. The journey there is an ongoing process, and I must keep going step by step, choice by choice.

Oh, how I sometimes wish there were an easy way to simplify my life! I would love for the Lord to rush in and whisk away my clutter, untangle my commitments, and overhaul my finances. I would love for him to miraculously change all the externals, giving me the instant simplicity and peace and order that I desire.

Instead, I am finding that his first priority is always to bring simplicity into my inner world. He wants me to keep making him the organizing principle in my life so that he can keep motivating and fueling my choices with his strong, calm sanity. And he wants me to trust him even before I can see any progress. He wants me to praise him even before I can see any results. And that's so different from the way I usually operate:

> We say show me and I'll trust you,
> He says trust me and I'll show you.
> That's the way he turns our hearts to his.
> We say change me and I'll praise you,
> He says praise me and I'll change you.
> That's the way the love of Jesus is.[6]

Reflecting on those old lyrics of mine reminds me of just how important it is to keep seeing with our hearts what our eyes cannot yet see. Seeing the simple, serene lives he wants to give us. The unrushed, unstressed days of tranquillity and peace that we yearn for but are not yet experiencing. It reminds me how important it is to keep making those small, simplifying choices one at a time, with his help.

This is what the Bible calls "walking by faith," and I

am convinced that it is the only way to travel to a place called Simplicity. The simpler, more balanced and serene life we're longing for is waiting for us at the end of a road paved with simplifying choices.

Clearing the Cluttered Path

4

In Its Own Sweet Time

*M*ost of us let ourselves slide into believing that someday...suddenly we'll have more time to do what we want or need to do. This passive "waiting until" attitude allows precious time to slip through our fingers like water to disappear forever.

—Dru Scott

❦

The time was 12:45 P.M. on a weekday in December, two years ago. My friend Jacque rushed into the crowded neighborhood deli twenty minutes later than our arranged meeting time. Her arms were loaded with holiday purchases, her brow was furrowed, and she had to perform a real balancing act to negotiate the distance between the door and our table. Dropping her load, she managed a last look at her watch before breathlessly flopping down in the chair next to mine.

"I hate being late!" she apologized. "But I can't seem to get anywhere on time any more. I'm always rushing. I feel like my life is on 'fast forward' and I can't find the stop button!"

I'm sure Jacque knew that if anyone could sympathize with her plight, it would be me. I had been feeling for months like a helpless victim of my own Daytimer.

Maybe you can relate to Jacque's feeling of frustration, too. Most of us have days when we feel we'll never get done all that needs doing, days when there seems to be a serious and mysterious shortage of that precious commodity, time. And though we hate feeling rushed and stressed out, it's a feeling we can't seem to avoid.

Boston Globe columnist Ellen Goodman has noted that one of the most requested items on "the American wish list" is "the longing for time":

> Ask families what they want and the same answer comes out: Time. Some tell the pollsters that they would exchange money for time, literally buy it if they could. Others express it in a desire to shortcut the complicated and unnatural cycle that takes them around the days like a stock car in an interminable race.

Slow Time, Fast Time, and "Time Out of Time"

Like the people in Ellen Goodman's column, I am often frustrated by a shortage of time. But something else about time puzzles me. The way I see it, there is time and there is time. Let me explain. I learned in school that there are sixty seconds in every minute, but it seems to me that some minutes go by at a totally different pace than others.

For instance, there are times when the clock seems to drag its feet or, more accurately, its hands. I recall a philosophy class I took one steamy summer in Louisiana, for instance, in which an hour could last all day. My seat was by the back door. In the hall outside, the deep

In Its Own Sweet Time

hum of a Coke machine motor would click on, providing a "white noise" backdrop for the lecture. The professor, a dapper, white-haired gentleman perpetually decked out in a moist-looking shirt and tie, would drone on and on in his soft, Southern "sing-song" that never failed to fill me with an intense longing for sleep. In fact, I remember thinking one day, "I would pay fifty dollars for a ten-minute nap!"

During these classes, time seemed to stand still. I would glance at my watch hundreds of times during the hour, only to find it had not progressed a notch. Each minute was an eternity.

Then there are the other kinds of days when time seems to speed up. This invariably happens to me on days when I have a long, detailed list of things to be done. I'll be rushing from here to there and back again, madly pushing to take care of my A-level commitments (fax first draft of musical to Dallas, take papers to tax man, attend worship committee meeting, pick up photos from Jane, get Spike's coat from cleaners, put roast in oven, meet Ann's plane at 4:15), hoping to get down to a few of my B-level commitments (take plant to Donna in hospital, do nails), and knowing full well that there will never be enough minutes in this lifetime to get to the Cs (register for creative writing class, learn Spanish in spare time).

On days like that, no matter how fast I move, I can't seem to come out ahead. I can summon all of my time-management tricks and techniques and still get the feeling I'm in a losing battle against the ticking clock and the draining hourglass. At the end of a day like that, I usually find that the minutes have run out before the As have been completed, the Bs have been considered, or the Cs have even been glanced at.

But there are other kinds of days—rare, mysterious days when I almost have the feeling that time has been suspended. They arrive unexpectedly, unbidden and unplanned. And when they do, it is almost as though I am lifted up and out of time on the wings of some lovely experience.

I remember particularly a James Taylor concert we attended one summer at the World's Fair in New Orleans. Seated in an open-air auditorium on the banks of the Mississippi River, we listened to J.T. and company perform all of our favorite songs to perfection. We could feel those old, familiar melodies moving through us while, just beyond the stage, huge, shadowy shapes of boats and barges moved through the muddy, moonlit water like great, oceangoing ghosts.

Just thinking about that experience still has the power to transport me. I couldn't tell you today how long the concert lasted. We seemed to be caught up somewhere outside the boundaries of ordinary hours, minutes, and seconds.

I remember another "time out of time" kind of day, an almost enchanted November afternoon years ago when my sister, Alix, and I sat out under the moss-draped oaks on my uncle's lawn in Thibodaux, Louisiana, watching our four little boys play in the autumn leaves. The sky was wide and blue, the air was clear and cool, and our children were wild with the joy of being alive. Again and again they would fall backward into the high, soft piles of leaves, laughing hysterically and squealing each other's names: "André and Curt and Andy and Marc! André and Curt and Andy and Marc!" We found ourselves laughing along with them, laughing until our sides ached. We lay on our backs looking up through the thick, woven pattern of the branches and felt the closeness of heaven somewhere behind the gentle blue covering of sky.

How long were we out on the lawn that day? Was it an hour or an afternoon? I couldn't say. The quality of what we shared seemed somehow to reach beyond the normal way we measure time.

Through the years of my life other times like that have come to me as special gifts of grace: a nature hike at Girl Scout day camp when I was nine . . . my first big role in the school operetta . . . a ride on the Staten Island ferry with our children . . . a weekday afternoon at the mall with Spike and a couple of crazy pals, "playing hooky" from work . . . a holiday dinner with four women friends in front of a huge, blazing fire . . . an amazing Sunday of worship and fellowship with the body of Christ at the Brooklyn Tabernacle (we were in church seven hours that June day in Brooklyn—three services—and it felt like an hour or two!) . . . a midnight vigil with Andy as we delivered a litter of mongrel pups . . . a picnic lunch with a dozen close friends on the grassy bald of a North Carolina mountaintop. What a joy to look back and gather up those lovely days like flowers for a bouquet.

Time in Greek

Whenever I try to describe what takes place during a "time out of time" kind of evening like the moonlit night of the James Taylor concert, or when I try to put words around an autumn afternoon like the one my sister and I spent with our children in the fallen leaves, I always have the feeling that our language lacks the needed words. There is no adequate way to describe or express in English the quality of a "time out of time" kind of time.

The Greek language is a little more helpful, however, because it has more than one word for time. *Chronos* is the Greek word for clock-controlled time. It is the root of our word *chronological*, and it describes the kind of time that is gauged by human measurement: by the hands of the clock and the pages of the calendar. It is the kind of time that Jacque was fighting with that December day when her life seemed to be caught in "fast forward."

In Its Own Sweet Time

Bills and term papers and taxes come due on *chronos* time. Monday mornings roll around with rigid regularity on *chronos* time. School, from the first day of first grade to the last diploma handed out on graduation day, runs on *chronos* time.

But there is another Greek word for what might be called "God-controlled time." That word is *kairos*, and it is the kind of time that we humans cannot gauge by clocks or calendars. With *kairos* time, God calls the shots. Flowers bloom on *kairos* time. Babies are born on *kairos* time. People fall in love and find life's deep meaning and have spiritual awakenings on *kairos* time.

Kairos time is measured by "moments" rather than by minutes. We can't push it or force it or hold it back. It will only happen when a heartbeat in heaven has decreed that the time is right.

At that riverside concert in New Orleans, caught up in the inner currents of sweet, familiar music, I am convinced I spent an evening on *kairos* time. On a long-ago autumn afternoon, beneath the grandeur of spreading oaks, drenched in sunshine and squeals of laughter, I feel certain that my sister and I were watching our children grow on *kairos* time. What's more, I would venture to say that most of the deeply meaningful, memorable, difficult-to-describe moments that I hold close to my heart have been *kairos* moments in time.

In my experience, people with a simple faith and a simple, childlike outlook seem to be more open to *kairos* moments. They are not so busy doing and achieving and creating their own self-constructed destiny that they miss the hidden treasures that are waiting in the ordinary events of life. And as I, too, seek a simpler life, it seems that my heart is learning to beat more in synch with those *kairos* moments. My eyes are becoming more open to the value of occasions and events that take place according to God's agenda. In the process, I believe I am

In Its Own Sweet Time

beginning to get the tiniest glimpse of what time will be like in heaven.

In heaven I believe that everything will have that lovely, suspended, "out of time" quality; we will be at home in eternity where there is no beginning and no end, and we will know it. We won't have to wear watches. No one will be rushing or pushing or meeting deadlines. We won't be trying to get to another appointment or another location. We'll all be right where we want to be, and we won't care to be anywhere else. Then, finally, we will know the sweet freedom of moving through life as it happens in its own sweet time.

More Time or More Meaning?

Thinking about time as either *chronos* (clock time) or *kairos* (God time) has got me wondering: Which kind of time are we really craving when we hunger for "more time"? Do we really want more clock time—more boring hours that never seem to pass, more frantic minutes to spend rushing around and racing against our deadlines? Or are we really hungering for more meaning-filled God time—more of the deep, sweet contentment that fills us when we are able to rest for a moment in the "timeless present"? Don't we really want more of the gentle, unhurried quality of life that we experience when we have freed ourselves to go with God's agenda?

And if it is indeed more God time we are longing for, where do we find it? How do we make more space for it in the crunch of our busy lives? How do we enter in?

Though we cannot manufacture a "*kairos* moment" (only God can do that!), I believe we *can* learn new ways to look at life that will encourage and invite the gift of a simpler, more spontaneous, less clock-driven way of life. We can make some subtle shifts in attitude that will welcome more meaning-filled experiences and relationships into our overplanned and overstressed lives, helping us settle into a place called Simplicity. Incorporating some of these *"kairos* principles" into our thinking about time is a good place to begin.

Learn to Live One Day at a Time

Jesus gave us the greatest clue to entering God time when he invited us to live and trust in this one day without jumping ahead to that great tangle of "what ifs" that wait to swallow us up when we start worrying about tomorrow.

> So do not worry, saying, "What shall we eat?" or "What shall we drink?" or "What shall we wear?" For the pagans run after all these things, and your heavenly Father knows that you need them. But seek first his kingdom and his righteousness, and all these things will be given to you as well. Therefore do not worry about tomorrow, for tomorrow will worry about itself. Each day has enough trouble of its own (Matthew 6:31-34).

I don't believe that Jesus was telling us to be foolish, thoughtless children who have no plans for earning a living or caring for our families. The book of Proverbs is full of pithy and pointed sayings that warn against laziness and procrastination. I believe that what he was saying, instead, is that we should avoid investing precious emotional energy in worrying over what is to come. We should make our plans, commit them to God, and then determine to receive today like a twenty-four-hour treasure to enjoy and celebrate.

But stewing over the past is every bit as harmful as worrying about the future. In fact, I have found it helpful to see the past and the future as two thieves that can rob us of the jewel of the "timeless present" by constantly pulling us backward or forward in time. This was the central idea I tried to express in my lyric "Between Two Thieves":

> The past will try to rob us of our peace of
> mind,
> The future tries to rob us of our faith,
> We can't go back to yesterday or catch up
> with tomorrow,
> Jesus, teach us how to live today.
>
> We're crucified between two thieves
> Named Yesterday and Tomorrow,
> Two thieves that try to steal our lives away.
> We're crucified between two thieves
> Named Yesterday and Tomorrow
> Until we learn to live our lives today.
>
> Help us to go on beyond our yesterdays
> And place tomorrow in your hands of grace,
> To give you all our past regret and all our
> future worry,
> To follow where your love will lead today.
>
> The lilies of the field bloom in the moment,
> The sparrows spread their wings and soar
> above;
> We can only live life to the fullest
> If we will live each moment in your sweet,
> eternal love.[1]

Why is constantly focusing on the past such a deadly outlook? Simply because we cannot change what has already happened, and so dwelling on past regrets is pointless and draining. There are no more useless words in the English language than the words *if only*. They consume all the energy we could spend on making our lives better today.

Focusing on the future is also deadly, because it is an invitation to worry. Worry contaminates the present moment more than almost any other activity, primarily because it precludes any possibility of faith in our lives.

Worry and faith are exact opposites and cannot coexist. Worry settles over our lives like a heavy blanket, allowing us to see only the negative possibilities in the future. Faith, on the other hand, lifts the heaviness from our hearts and opens our eyes to see and believe in the positive possibilities the future holds. It allows us to let God hold tomorrow until we get to it.

Choosing to release the past to God's redemptive grace and trust the future to God's faithfulness simplifies our lives because it rids our hearts of past regrets and future worries. It can also bring a tremendous flow of energy and freedom into our lives as it returns to us the beauty of the present moment. Like Ebenezer Scrooge after his awful Christmas Eve journeys into the regrets of the past and the fears of the future, we can wake up into the glorious sunshine of this one morning realizing that it's not too late! We still have today, and we can begin to make it count!

Make the Most of the Time You Have

I have talked for years about "making more time" for relaxation or "making time" for some activity or another. But the simple, freeing truth I am learning to enjoy is that I cannot *make* time. I cannot manufacture any amount of it or buy any quantity of it or make any more of it than there already is. I can only make the most of the amount that I have been given.

In Genesis we are told who thought up time and brought it into being. That is the place where God said, "Let there be lights in the expanse of the sky to separate the day from the night, and let them serve as signs to mark seasons and days and years" (Genesis 1:14).

God, in other words, is the creator of time. None of us can make a day or a night or a season or an extra second. That is in God's job description and not in ours. What's more, everyone in this world gets the same amount of time. I have twenty-four hours in my day, exactly the same as the president of the United States and Mother Teresa and the checkout person at the grocery store.

The question, therefore, is not how much more time I need, but what am I going to do with the amount I have already been given.

Scripture advises us in Ephesians 5:16 and later in Colossians 4:5 to live wisely by "making the most of every opportunity." Considering those scriptural admonitions, I can't help wondering what kind of accounting we will have to give regarding our use of time when we get to heaven.

Will God show us an "instant replay" of all the meaning-filled *kairos* moments we embraced and made time for? Will we see flashing before our eyes all the times we spent getting to know each other and God, finding joy in our work, sharing our possessions, telling good news, marveling at sunsets and sunrises, laughing with children, stopping to care for old people, praying with friends? Or will God merely sigh and pull out a huge stack of all the scratched-out "to do" lists we carried around day in and day out? I pray that those dictatorial little lists will not be the sum and summary of my life! God, help me make the most of the time that I've been given!

Don't Wait to Be Happy

I remember thinking when my big sister Alix got married that now her life would be total bliss. (I was seventeen years old at the time and a hopeless romantic.) Instead, the early years of her marriage were what most early marriages are: something of a struggle. Her husband was an intern earning just enough money at the hospital to make ends meet. They had two small children and lived in a tiny New Orleans apartment.

For Alix's birthday one year, Mom and Dad sent her money to buy a new winter coat. She carefully shopped and picked out a well-made, black-wool overcoat that fit her perfectly. There was only one thing wrong. Black is not a good color on Alix.

"Why black?" Mom asked.

"Oh," she explained, "I looked better in the red one, but I wanted something practical. We have to be practical. There will be plenty of time for red coats when we are out of this internship and making more money."

It didn't take Alix long to recognize her mistake. Though the black coat did last and last, it never brought her any joy. It was a super-sensible, overly practical, dismal reminder of their daily struggle to get by.

"If there was ever a time for a red coat, it was that year," she later realized. "It would have lasted every bit as long, and every time I wore it, it would have given my spirits a lift."

Do we have more *kairos* moments in red coats? I can't say for certain, but I do suspect that the heart that feels free enough to choose a spirit-lifting, bright-red coat even in the face of financial struggles is a heart that is open to present-moment joy.

It is a common misconception that "later on" we will finally be able to be happy—after a certain goal is reached or certain circumstances are changed. The simple truth is that happiness is a learned behavior and it takes most of us a lifetime to get the knack of it. There is only one time to begin learning how to appropriate the joy that is all around us, and that time is today!

Trust That There Will Be Time Enough

Here is a simple revelation that is bringing me a lot of freedom: There *is* enough time. As I am learning to move with the rhythm of God's *kairos* agenda, I am discovering that I have exactly the right number of hours and minutes and seconds to accomplish and do everything that I need to do in my lifetime.

That doesn't mean that every item on my list will get marked off neatly and completely. It doesn't mean that everything I want to do will get done. But it does mean that God will help me discern what things will be most meaningful to me and most important to him and that, once I've determined what they are, he will help me find the time to do them. As the beautiful book of Ecclesiastes puts it:

> There is a right time for everything:
>
> A time to be born, A time to die;
> A time to plant; A time to harvest;
> A time to kill; A time to heal;
> A time to destroy; A time to rebuild;
> A time to cry; A time to laugh;
> A time to grieve; A time to dance;
> A time for scattering stones; A time for
>   gathering stones;
> A time to hug; A time not to hug;
> A time to find; A time to lose;
> A time for keeping; A time for throwing
>   away;
> A time to tear; A time to repair;
> A time to be quiet; A time to speak up;
> A time for loving; A time for hating;
> A time for war; A time for peace.
> (Ecclesiastes 3:1-8 TLB)

Spend "Saved Time" on What Is Meaningful

What would you do with more time if you actually had it? Think carefully about that question.

For years I sought out as many "time expanding" techniques as I could, assuming that I would pack all

73

those extra hours I saved with fun or restful or meaning-ful activities. But I found instead that rushing around "saving time" had somehow become addictive. Instead of using the time I had saved to rest and reflect and enjoy my relationships, I found myself using it to cram more achievements and activities into the hours I had saved!

Ralph Keyes, author of the time-management book, *Timelock*, discovered the same sort of irony when he researched the effect of labor-saving devices on the lives of busy people. He found that many of these devices that had been designed to simplify and relax the stressed and the overcommitted are, in actuality, only encouraging the already overworked to work more:

> Power mowers give us less excuses for not cutting the grass. Blow dryers let us wash our hair daily! Dustbusters make it possible to suck dirt regularly from spaces vacuum cleaners can't reach. Washer-dryers allow us to do laundry constantly rather than weekly.[2]

To combat this tendency, Keyes suggests that we must focus on "what we want from life (as opposed to how much we can 'get done')" before we will ever be able to make any significant changes in the way we use time. He suggests the following checklist for evaluating time use:

- Think regularly about what you want from your life.

- Evaluate all activities, even the most trivial, by whether they add to that life.

- Ruthlessly weed out whatever does not— tasks, errands, TV shows, people.[3]

What a pity it would be to get to the end of our lives and realize that we had rushed around for years only to make more time available for more rushing around! How much better to spend our extra, bonus hours on what is most meaningful to us.

Locate and Eliminate Your
Meaningless "Time Gobblers"

Have you ever found yourself thinking that there is a conspiracy out there of people and activities bent on eating up your precious hours? If you are anything like me, you probably have some "time gobblers" operating in your life. Time gobblers are all those meaningless habits and pastimes that daily chew up and swallow our precious time—filling our days without really contributing to our lives in any way.

These pursuits don't have to be evil or sinful to do us harm (most of them aren't). All they have to do is distract us long enough to take us away from the really meaningful and important things in our lives. But just identifying what they are can put us on the alert and help us fight back. For instance, among the time gobblers I've been gradually trying to weed out of my own life are gabbing for too long on the telephone; mindless television watching (flipping the channels and taking potluck); and "shopping" in catalogs that arrive in the mailbox, even when I know I don't need or intend to buy anything. Other time gobblers might be playing too many computer games, reading magazines, or rearranging knickknacks.

One way to fight a time gobbler is to consider what you might do with the hours you would save should you decide to give your "gobbler" up. David Wilkerson in his book, *The Cross and the Switchblade*, tells about an evening when he felt bored and restless with his nightly time-gobbling habit of watching television:

> "How much time do I spend in front of that screen each night?" I wondered. "A couple

of hours at least. What would happen, Lord, if I sold that TV set and spent that time—praying?" I was the only one in the family who ever watched TV anyway. What would happen if I spent two hours every single night in prayer? It was an exhilarating idea. Substitute prayer for television, and see what happened.[4]

The account of Wilkerson's sale of his TV set, his adventure with prayer, and his subsequent journey into the strange and dangerous world of teenage gangs is the exciting story of the founding of Teen Challenge. David Wilkerson's decision to eliminate his personal time gobbler opened a window of time in his life that led to the founding of a worldwide ministry for inner city youth.

Now, I am not saying you have to rush out and found a worldwide ministry with the time you wrest from your time gobbler. I am not even suggesting that you pack every hour and minute with "useful" activities. You might choose to spend your saved time just relaxing. In fact, some of my most precious *kairos* moments have come when I'm just sitting around "doing nothing" with people I love. What I am talking about is weeding out the kind of pursuits that eat up time without really bringing rest or renewal. Getting rid of those habitual, time-wasting activities can open up amazing stores of time to spend on what is truly meaningful to you.

Enjoy the Journey

In her bestselling book, *Downshifting*, Amy Saltzman tells of meeting a friend, a busy, professional woman like herself, for a long-overdue visit. As Amy confided to her friend a recent decision she had made to "take life a little slower" by spending more time on herself and her

In Its Own Sweet Time

relationships she realized that her friend was staring at her with a puzzled expression, totally baffled by Amy's shared confidence. And then Amy realized that most of her success-oriented friends would have trouble relating to anything besides working hard to reach their goals in life: "If we weren't always moving ahead and aiming for something higher and more impressive, if we didn't have that look of constantly being busy and in motion, we were somehow boring or even losers."[5]

Everybody needs purposes and goals in life. But there is little room for *kairos* moments in the life that is totally goal oriented, totally geared toward moving ahead. Every day, every hour, every minute is carefully scheduled to yield a certain reward: success, power, money. Every step is directed to arrive at a certain destination, carefully moving the life from point A to point B to point C, onward and upward.

The world of the success seeker definitely turns on *chronos* time. That is why I believe the heart that is hungry for more meaning, the life that is longing for more God-controlled *kairos* moments, must consciously choose to slow down, to stop rushing, to stop focusing only on the destination and begin enjoying the journey.

Toward the end of his ministry, Jesus had a specific destination upon which he was focused. Luke 9:51 says that "he stedfastly set his face to go to Jerusalem" (KJV). But as he journeyed, Jesus still flowed with the currents of *kairos* time. He took time out on the way to talk with his friends, to share a meal, to meet new people. On his way to heal one person, Jesus was sometimes stopped by an appeal to heal another. He was constantly keeping his spiritual eyes open to catch a vision of God's agenda rather than pigheadedly pursuing some plan of his own. He knew who he was in relation to the Father, and his life moved according to that awareness.

I love Karla Worley's insight on Jesus' agenda: "I don't think he kept a 'to do' list. ('Heal blind man, 11:30;

In Its Own Sweet Time

cast out demon, 2:15; Monday: stop by temple and rebuke Pharisees.') I think he just was who he was."[6] Jesus was a man who welcomed interruptions as part of the big scheme of things—a man who found a way to embrace unplanned-for possibilities, meet present needs, and rejoice in the unexpected beauty of the moment without in any way compromising the imperatives of his major goal. And I truly believe he calls us to do the same: to travel with a purpose, but to live as fully as possible all the way to our destination.

Learn to Waste Time with Abandon

Many of us know that it would be best for our health and our happiness if we slowed down. But those of us who have bought into the work ethic of our success-driven culture have difficulty making a conscious choice to do so. Slowing down, being still, acting spontaneously, welcoming the unscheduled in life—we find these things very difficult.

One of the most helpful pieces of advice I ever received on this subject of slowing down was given to me at a retreat led by Father Francis Vanderwall more than a dozen years ago. "We must give ourselves permission," Francis said, "to waste time with God. Just as two lovers are content to sit in silence and just 'be' together, so must we learn to just be with the One who loves us most. What feels to the Western mind like a waste of time can actually be the most valuable investment of time. But in order to soothe our restless and goal-oriented spirits, we must simply say to ourselves . . . 'Yes! Today I choose to waste time with Jesus!'"

I have used this wonderful advice for other precious investments of my time in *kairos* moments. This March, when a snowstorm covered the entire eastern side of the United States, it left even our little part of the Alabama

Gulf Coast as white and snow-covered as a Christmas-card picture. As thrilled as I was to see the beautiful snow (which we very rarely see in this part of the world), I was less than thrilled with its timing. I had promised myself I would spend the day working on my Simplicity book.

When our friends Jandy and Sonny called to ask if they could come by and have a picnic in the snow with us, the workaholic in me said, "We'd love to see you. But why don't you come by this afternoon? I have to work this morning."

As I brought up the words of my book on the computer screen and read a few paragraphs about my decision to make simpler, less-driven choices, I had to laugh out loud. Was I really planning to spend the only snowy day in six years sitting behind a word processor and writing about how to embrace the special, unplanned for moments in life? So I called Jandy and Sonny back, and the four of us had a special *kairos* kind of morning!

Time is a special gift, priceless and irreplaceable. We cannot make it; we can only make the most of it, today. And today the April air is clear and sweet outside my window. A breeze is playing games in and out of the pine and juniper needles, and Frodo, my furry haystack of a dog, keeps dropping his tennis ball on the porch floor just outside my office door, begging me for a game of fetch.

The *chronos* reading on my black, plastic, digital Ironman watch is "4:35." But the *kairos* beating of my heart is telling me to turn this Macintosh off for the afternoon. If I open my spiritual eyes, I just might discover a "moment" out there waiting for me to claim it!

5

The House We Call Home

I pass a lot of houses on my way home. Some pretty, some expensive, some inviting. But my heart always skips a beat when I turn down the road and see my house nestled against the hill.

—Bob Benson

❦

On a summer afternoon the year I turned twelve, my friend Dolcie Dean and I found a deserted shack in a field near her house. The walls were weathered and thin and papered with pictures torn from magazines and calendars. The floors were covered with dirt, and you could see patches of sky through the roof. There was nothing much in the old place but a couple of broken chairs and a few old apple crates. But it was a house—a little house that no one lived in—and we were as thrilled with it as if it had been a mansion. We decided to adopt it like a stray puppy and make it our own.

Afraid of what Dolcie's mother might say if we actually asked her about the shack, we gathered our supplies from her house like a couple of cat burglars. We rounded up sheets for curtains, bottles for vases, a little stash of drinks and sandwich fixings for energy, and some cleaning supplies. The rest of that afternoon and all the next day we worked feverishly on our little house, cleaning and arranging and "decorating."

The whole time we worked, we were planning all the wonderful things we would do now that we had our very own house. We discussed the selective membership of the club we would form to meet here. We planned the kinds of parties we would have and who would be invited. We even considered buying a horse that we could keep in the field outside (after we had built a fence, of course).

By late afternoon of the second day, our little house looked adorable. We had swept out mountains of dirt. We had fashioned and hung bedsheet curtains at the paneless windows. Empty pop bottles with beautiful wildflower arrangements covered every available surface. And our heads were filled with elaborate dreams that centered around our little "cottage in the meadow."

But little did we know, as we were standing back and admiring our handiwork, that Dolcie's mother was frantically calling everyone she knew, asking if anyone had seen us. We had been gone since early morning. She had no idea where we were. And now it was beginning to get dark.

Finally, she sent Dolcie's father (a huge, handsome man who was the football coach at our local university) out to look for us. He spied us crossing the field in front of our hideout. Sadly, that was the beginning of the end of all our dreams.

Dolcie's parents explained to us that we had been trespassing on property that had been purchased by a real-estate developer and was soon to be turned into a subdivision. Our little house was already scheduled to be torn down, and furthermore it was very dangerous to play around old, empty houses, and first thing in the morning we would have to go and retrieve all of our belongings and never, no never, no never go back there again.

An Excitement Awakened

Even though my first experience as a "homeowner" did not have a happy ending, it awakened in me an excitement I've felt ever since about fixing up a place of my own.

Spike and I have lived in a number of homes before this little log cabin: a tiny, tidy bungalow we inhabited when we were struggling married students; a drafty duplex in New Orleans within earshot of the rumbling St. Charles Avenue streetcar; a roomy (though elderly) family home on a shady street where our children were babies. And there was the comfortable brick house in Mobile where we spent most of the last twenty years of our lives—a home with lots of living space, closets, neighbors, and other features that I didn't adequately appreciate until this year, when I tried living without them!

That house will always be special to me, mainly because I raised my children there. And I'll have to admit that though my mind and my spirit were prepared to leave it when we moved to this little cabin in the woods, my heart was much more difficult to transplant.

An Issue of the Heart

Loving a house is like any other kind of love. It is not a rational matter, but more a matter of the heart. Writer Phyllis McGinley, reminiscing about buying her first home, wrote, "The right house, no matter what its period, must pluck you by the sleeve and say, 'Take me. We were meant for each other.'"[1] It's like love at first sight.

But eventually our feelings for a home will go beyond that first attraction. Deeper feelings will develop. If the

The House We Call Home

times we have spent there have been mainly positive and nurturing, then our heart attitude and our feelings toward that place will be warm and good. If our times there have been a mixture of happiness, pain, and sadness, those emotions will color our feelings about the house.

One of my very favorites of the choir musicals I've written is *Love Will Be Our Home*, which I was privileged to create with my friend, Nancy Gordon. There is a song near the opening of the musical entitled, "The House We Call Home." It begins with these words:

> It's just a house on a street in a town,
> It may not look special to you,
> But this is the house where we lived and we
>   loved,
> Where we slept and we ate and we grew.[2]

In several of the performances that I saw of the musical, this particular song was used as a musical backdrop for a slide presentation. As the emotional words and melody were performed by the choir, pictures of different family homes were flashed on screens around the church auditorium. One church even used slides of the actual childhood homes of many church members who were in the audience. The emotional reaction of those church members upon seeing their childhood homes flash before their eyes was intense. One woman loudly blurted out, "That was our house!" and several others were wiping tears from their eyes.

Homes Have Personalities

I think during that performance I realized something I have known but never quite put into words before—that homes have personalities just like people. In fact, the personality of the home is almost always a reflection of the people who live there. If the people are

The House We Call Home

happy and relaxed and feeling pretty great about life, then the home they live in will take on that personality and will probably be a delightful place to live in and to visit.

I remember the times that I went with my mother-in-law to visit her dear friend, Sue. Sue had seven children and was not an extremely organized type. Usually an assortment of trikes, dolls, and toys in various sizes were scattered throughout the house. There was invariably a stack of ironing piled in a chair and evidence of some meal either coming or going on the table, stove, or sink.

But what impressed me most about Sue's home was the warm and gracious welcome we always received there. Sue never seemed the least bit self-conscious about the condition of her home. She was never apologetic. She would squeal with delight at the sight of us, scoop a stack of toys or laundry off of a couple of chairs so that we could sit down, and then spend a comfortable, wonderful hour or more chatting and visiting, undaunted by the frequent interruptions of her children. The atmosphere of Sue's home said, "Come in and be part of our family! You're welcome here!"

Sue's hospitable home was very different indeed from the home of a woman I'll call Gail whom we knew briefly while we were stationed at Fort Knox, Kentucky, during the 1960s. Since both of our husbands were second lieutenants, Gail and I lived in identical quarters with the exact same floor plan. But Gail's house didn't look much like mine most of the time! It was always *immaculate*. There was never the slightest suggestion of dust or disorder. Her yard was immaculate. Her car was immaculate. Her makeup was immaculate. Even her two-year-old was immaculate, because Gail was always able to catch any spit-up in midair before it hit the baby's coveralls!

I never felt at home in Gail's house. To tell you the truth, I don't think that *Gail* ever felt at home in Gail's house. She was on twenty-four-hour patrol against the

The House We Call Home

smallest sign of incipient dirt or clutter. While you were trying to explain something to her, she was plumping pillows and straightening pictures, and sometimes I'd look up to find that she was washing my glass before I had even finished drinking out of it! I finally got to the point that I just figured my friendship was too much trouble for Gail, and I stopped going over there.

The Simplicity Hall of Fame

From the descriptions of these two homes, which would you say has the simplest and most serene atmosphere? Like many questions about simplicity, the answer to that question is a bit complicated. Compared to the disorder and outer confusion of Sue's home, Gail's clean, orderly domicile might appear at first glance to win hands down. On the other hand, if genuine simplicity and serenity start on the inside, then Sue would be the winner.

But probably neither of the two homes described above would win a spot in the Simplicity Hall of Fame. Both of them have good points, and both have bad points. Though I'd prefer to be around Sue's personality type any day, I'm afraid the degree of disorder in her home would be a little overwhelming, even for me. And as much as I would appreciate Gail's orderly closets and shiny tabletops, I'm afraid her neatnik perfectionism would have my insides tied in knots if I had to spend much time in her home.

Arriving at a Balance

Thinking about Sue's good-natured confusion and Gail's rigid fastidiousness left me pondering: How do we arrive at the kind of balance in our home's "personality" that will make it a place of genuine simplicity and serenity? What is a simple home? What needs does it meet? What does it look like and how does it feel? Here are some ideas I've discovered in my pondering.

A Simple Home Exists for People

I realize it may sound pretty elementary to begin by saying that simple homes exist for people. But some homes I have been in (like Gail's, for instance) have seemed to be in control of the people who live in them rather than the other way around. Functioning as slave drivers, these homes "crack the whip" over the householder, driving them to scrub and straighten and polish and live in bondage to the building that they are supposed to possess. I have seen other houses that almost seemed to be out of control—so messy and cluttered that the family almost had to "live around them" instead of in them.

A home is only valuable if it "serves" the family that lives in it. It should be a *means* to a more fulfilling life, not an *end* in itself. If our homes are taking time and money and attention and energy away from the people in our families, then they are out of balance. If we are spending our time refinishing floors instead of going to a child's T-ball game, for instance, something is badly out of whack. If the money we should be spending on the needs of the people we love is being spent instead to make our homes into showplaces, then we are indeed in bondage to a building.

Simple Homes Have an Authentic Personality

The homes that I enjoy the most have less to do with architecture and decor and more to do with authenticity. A home feels simple and unified and whole to me when it speaks with the accents of the people who live there. A home that expresses the character, tastes, and values of the people who live in it is authentic whether it be sleek and modern, rustic and homey, ruffled and charming, or spare and graceful.

In authentic homes I never get the feeling that I am visiting a showplace. Instead, I feel that I am visiting the heart and substance of a human personality. What a difference!

My great-aunt Ada's home in New Orleans had galleries and porch swings and claw-footed bathtubs and a wonderful array of her "memories" on the walls and tabletops. It may not have looked simple in the classic sense, but it was a home that "knew who it was." Each vase or candlestick or framed photograph held for my great-aunt a treasured part of her past, and she delighted in telling my sisters and me the story behind each. How we loved visiting in Aunt Ada's home—because it was such an authentic expression of who she was.

One home that Spike and I felt privileged to visit when we were college students was the home of our English professors, Drs. Milton and Patricia Rickles. At the end of each semester, they would invite their classes out to their home on the river for a farewell party. The humor and intelligence of our hosts could be felt in every room of their home. Comfortable sofas and colorful rugs and walls of bookshelves bulging with books created an inviting atmosphere. There were always huge trays of fruit and cheese, and at some point during the evening someone would read a paper or an original poem or story. I think back on those occasions with delight and can't help wondering, looking around at my own book-filled house on the river, just how much Spike and I were influenced by those special evenings.

I admire the character Tess Hayes in Vicki Covington's novel *Night Ride Home* for her ability to infuse the bleak, colorless "company house" she shares with her coal-miner husband into something artful and aesthetically pleasing. In this scene from the book, Bolivia, a neighbor, sees Tess's house for the first time:

> Bolivia stood at the door, taking in the Hayes' place. The walls were freshly painted, the

same color as the eggshells in Bolivia's basket. Tess's drapes were lightweight and ivory colored rather than olive drab. The red-hot coals in the fireplace cast a warmth over the entire room. Beside the table was a modest buffet where clay pots painted a rainbow of colors held sprigs of magnolia leaves. And there was a piano. It was hard to believe this was a company house.[3]

Homes that express our uniqueness will not be decorated by following the instructions from a magazine ad or by taking a trip to a furniture store. They will grow out of the soil of our circumstances and bloom like our personalities over a period of time.

How can we make our homes into authentic expressions of who we are? Doris Longacre suggests we begin by asking "Who are we?" and "What will we do in this room?" Answering these questions can give us important clues to help us find our home's unique character. For instance, they can help us decide whether a room's furnishings should be formal or relaxed and whether the color scheme should be peaceful and relaxing or bright and stimulating. In the process, they can help insure that the decor of each room enhances the purposes and personalities of the people who live in them.[4]

Simple Homes Nurture Our Needs

Each of us has basic needs for rest and shelter, nourishment and love. Our homes should be places that help us meet those needs as simply and forthrightly as possible.

The simple home, in other words, is a nurturing home. It is, literally and figuratively, a safe and comfortable place to "come in from the storms of life." It is a

The House We Call Home

place where we know we'll get fed, physically and spiritually—a place where we are allowed to kick our shoes off, put our feet up, and be ourselves.

When our friend Eileen first laid eyes on her ranch-style home in Eugene, Oregon, it was the living room she fell in love with. That room was spacious and bright and, best of all, there was a fireplace and lots of bookcases. After purchasing the house, Eileen prepared to move her furniture in. But every time she tried to picture her bedroom furniture in one of the three bedrooms, which were small and located at the back of the house, Eileen felt cheated and depressed. She realized she really wanted to spend all of her time in the living room. And in the end, that is exactly what she decided to do! She used the roomy den/kitchen combination for her main living area and made her beautiful living room into the kind of bedroom she enjoys every single day.

Interior designer Alexandra Stoddard would applaud Eileen's decision. Stoddard discourages her clients from concentrating their energies "on things that are for special occasions rather than on the things we do, or use, every day." She feels that when people spend the most time, attention, and money decorating the parts of the home they use daily (the kitchen, the bedroom, and the bath) they are making wise choices to enhance and celebrate their everyday lives.[5]

Simple Homes Contain the Essential and the Significant

Time is short and life is precious. Who among us has excess minutes or hours to spend on what is nonessential or insignificant? And yet our homes (our closets, our desks, our dresser drawers, our attics and basements) are usually cluttered with unneeded items that consume precious time, space, and energy.

Author and cleaning expert Don Aslett found out how widespread a problem "clutter and junk" pose for people when he included one chapter on "decluttering" in his book, *Is There Life After Housework?* In more than six hundred radio and television interviews promoting the book, the majority of the questions he received from call-in audiences were on this subject of dejunking.

Based on some of those interviews and the huge amount of mail he also got on the subject, Aslett concluded that clutter is one of the biggest reasons for personal unhappiness in this country. "I discovered that people suffered acute guilt and actual damage from the junk that clutters their lives," he said.[6]

When Spike and I cleaned out our house in Mobile in preparation for our move to the country, we made the decision to give away or sell much of what we owned, keeping only what we really needed (the essential) or highly treasured (the significant). It seemed that every closet and drawer and corner of the attic contained stacks of nonessential and/or insignificant things. Although I cannot say that this process of "stripping down" was easy or painless, I can tell you that it was tremendously liberating. As we pulled away from Mobile with what remained of our possessions loaded into only one small private mover's truck, I felt as if I had lost a thousand pounds. Actually, I had!

One rationale that helped me find the courage to get rid of so much excess baggage was this: I convinced myself that I was trading these possessions for something I treasured much more—space. Not only physical space, but spiritual and emotional space. The space I was gaining by decluttering brought with it a peace and serenity and simplicity that made parting with my things possible.

Anne Morrow Lindbergh made this acute observation about space:

> It is only framed in space that beauty blooms.
> Only in space are events and objects and

people unique and significant—and therefore beautiful. A tree has significance if one sees it against the empty face of the sky. A note in music gains significance from the silences on either side. . . . Even small and casual things take on significance if they are washed in space.[7]

The many things I parted with when I left Mobile have left a blessed space around the few things I have chosen to keep. For instance, I once had many china platters. Now I have one large one and one small one. Both are beautiful and special to me. They are *essential* for serving my food. And they are *significant*, because they are the two of which I was fondest, the two I treasured enough to keep.

Simple Homes Are Shared

A home is truly a blessing in this unwelcoming world, a treasure more precious than we realize! So many in the world will fall asleep tonight without a bed or a pillow or a roof over their heads. We are told in Scripture that Jesus, the Son of Man, had "no place to lay his head" (Luke 9:58). And yet how often we take our homes for granted.

Whatever home we have been blessed to own or rent or otherwise inhabit is quite simply a gift, and the simple-hearted among us realize that good gifts are meant to be shared. Our homes should stand ready to welcome friends, kin, strangers, and pilgrims; lonely people, misfits, people needing healing, people hungry for friendship, and people needing to know the Lord.

When I was growing up, my mom and dad had a tiny guest room and bath on the first floor of our house which was often inhabited by some young man or woman who was temporarily without a place to go. One young woman stayed for three years, "coming home" to my parents' house until she finished college and had a house of her own!

We love to visit in the home of our friends, the Yearwoods, who have a beautiful gift of hospitality. Tom and Lisa are constantly opening their home to different groups and gatherings, and they have a wonderful way of caring for and listening to each guest, making each one feel that he is the most interesting and important person in the room.

Karen Mains's book *Open Heart, Open Home* puts forth a wonderful philosophy of hospitality. She makes the clear distinction between "entertaining," which is a way of glorifying the hostess, and "hospitality," which is a way of honoring the guest. Our world is in desperate need of little havens of hospitality where our faith, our food, and our friendship are available to those who need it.

Simple Homes Have a Ministry

Simple homes are gracious places that have a ministry of their own in much the same way that people do. For example, the home of our friend Annie Hunt has a distinct ministry of joy. The wonderful, eclectic blend of furnishings, the colorful artwork, the framed photographs of Annie's children and grandchildren on every tabletop combine with the radiant personality of the hostess to present each guest with the gift of joy.

Susan and F.G. Baldwin's home in Mobile has the ministry of prayer. Prayer in that home flows as easily as tap water! During our son Andy's difficult and rebellious teenage years, many prayers for him went up from that beautiful, gracious, and faith-filled home. And most of them were answered!

Our cabin has a ministry of rest and refreshment. People tend to drop their worry and compulsion up at the front gate, and by the time they travel the quarter mile to the house, their tension has begun to unwind. My friend Mimi, who is a bundle of energy and activity in other settings, always looks forward to her naps at our cabin. Our friends Pam and Mike Rozelle, whose unique ministry keeps them on the road much of the year, plan periodic "pit stops" here at Juniper Landing to soak up some of the rest and refreshment that is so abundant in this setting.

The Mobile home of our friends Conlee and Signa has a wonderful ministry of fellowship which we are often privileged to enjoy. Their house is always filled with delicious smells from the kitchen and interesting guests. Good conversation and laughter are built into the times around their table.

Perhaps you've never thought of your house as having a ministry. But I'll bet it does—or if it doesn't yet, it could and should. Tell the Lord that you realize your home is a gift from him and that you would like to see it have a ministry all its own. Volunteer to use it for his kingdom in whatever way he would show you, and then be listening for his answer to that prayer!

Simple Homes Have a Conscience

However personal and private our homes may be, they do not exist in a vacuum. They exist as part of a neighborhood, a community, a country, and a world. As men and women committed to finding a simpler life, we can't ignore the fact that luxuries and indulgences in our homes may be compromising the basic needs and rights of others. The way we use utilities and other natural resources in our homes affects our neighbors not only next door but around the world. What we eat matters. The way we dispose of our garbage and trash makes a difference.

Like it or not, we must face the fact that the many

simple choices we make in our homes every day can affect our world either positively or negatively. Something as small as choosing to put on a sweater when we're cold instead of reaching for the thermostat actually has global implications. The way we view the poor of the world, whether as brothers and sisters or as the opposite side of a "them and us" equation, is a key consideration.

Seeing to it that my home has a conscience is one way of being sensitive to these words from 1 John 3:17: "But whoever has the world's goods, and beholds his brother in need and closes his heart against him, how does the love of God abide in him?" (NASB).

I'll have to admit, however, that I'm tired of being made to feel guilty about being "comfortable" (most of the world would call it "rich"), wasteful, and an American, although I'll confess to being all of those things. I am so grateful for books like Doris Longacre's *Living More with Less*, which encourage me rather than scolding me. This wonderful little book (and there are others like it) encourages me to live more responsibly by teaching me small but specific ways my home can exist in better harmony with the world community.[8]

Simple Homes Are "Tents"

Our friends Jacque and Phillip have moved seventeen times in twenty-nine years of marriage! I wonder if that is some kind of a record. Jacque hates moving, and I know how she feels; even though I haven't had as much experience as she has, I hate it, too. I resent having my nest upset. I'd like to get everything set and settled and decorated and gather the people I love around me and just stay put.

But there is some good news and some bad news about that prospect. The bad news first: Nobody gets to stay put. This world we're in is in the process of passing away, and no matter where our earthly home is located, all of us are eventually going to have to "move."

And the good news? The good news is that the ultimate home to which God is calling us (through his son, Jesus) is about as permanent as you can get! This is the home that our hearts are really longing for. It's the capital-letter Home that lasts throughout capital-letter Eternity.

As Doris Longacre reminds us, "No inheritance, real estate settlement, or faultless house plan fully answers the cry for roots. Christians consciously travel toward a better housing development—a home in the city 'whose builder and maker is God.'"[9]

Just like our spiritual forebears, Abraham and Sarah, in the desert, we need to think with the minds of tent dwellers where our homes are concerned. We need to constantly keep in mind that as long as we are on this planet, we are not going to be permanently settled. And learning to see our homes as temporary and "hold them lightly" is one very simple way of lining up with God's viewpoint.

Simple Homes Make a Connection with Nature

Marjorie Kinnan Rawlings in her classic book, *Cross Creek*, says that we human beings "cannot live without the earth or apart from it, and something is shriveled in a man's heart when he turns away from it and concerns himself only with the affairs of men."[10]

Simple homes are not inhabited by folk with shriveled hearts. Whether by way of a bountiful backyard vegetable garden, a flowerpot on a city windowsill, or even a beautiful landscape on the wall, almost every simple home has found a way to connect with nature. Simple homes exist in harmony with the creation of which they are a part. Simple homes are places where things and people bloom and grow side by side.

The greatest change in my heart and attitude since my move to this country cabin has been an opening up of my eyes and mind and heart and spirit to my natural surroundings. I am comforted by the beauty of this place; I am inspired by it; I am quieted and healed by it.

Spike's poem "Elixir," written here at Juniper Landing, speaks movingly of the way we are healed by the calmness and the colors of our country home:

> Go amongst the waters here.
> Shape yourself against the winds.
> Measure their flow by your surfaces.
> limb by liquid—skin by tempest,
> Balm for the body.
>
> Take on some golden here.
> Bind yourself to purple and green.
> Breathe deep of dark red and brown.
> sunlight—petal—feather—leaf,
> Salve for the spirit.
>
> Fill your hollows with some music here.
> Set your ear to its simple voices,
> Resonant of change, a-hum with life.
> sky and earth song—bird and brook song,
> Medicine for the soul.[11]

—Robert A. Cloninger

A Dream of Simplicity

My own personal ideal of a simple home is not yet a reality, but it's much closer to coming true than ever before. I am nearer now than ever to knowing what a simple home means and what I want my little cabin in the clearing to be like.

I found strong elements of that dream of mine recently in some of the writings of an early naturalist named John Burroughs, who said:

> For my part, as I grow older, I am more and more inclined to reduce my baggage, to lop off superfluities. I become more and more in love with simple things and simple folk—a small house, a hut in the woods, a tent on the shore. The show and splendor of great houses, elaborate furnishings, stately halls, oppress me, impose upon me. They fix the attention upon false values, they set up a false standard of beauty: They stand between me and the real feeders of character and thought.[12]

Like Burroughs, the homes that I admire are simple ones. They are the homes that exist for people and nurture their needs; homes that have a personality, a ministry and a conscience; homes that are stripped of clutter and shared with others. And though their roots are sunk deep into the beauty of this earthly creation, still they are seen by those who love them as temporary dwellings standing in the light of an Eternal Home. These are the kinds of homes that open doors of simplicity and serenity to all who live and all who visit in them.

6

Money, Malls, and Moth Teeth

*T*he average person in our country is three weeks away from bankruptcy. He has little or no money saved, regular fixed obligations to support a relatively high lifestyle, significant monthly credit obligations and a total dependence on next week's paycheck to keep the budget afloat.

—Crown Ministries
Financial Study

❧

My friend Margaret[1] called just before lunch today. We haven't seen each other in about three months, so it took us thirty minutes or more to catch up on all the latest about our families, our work, and our lives.

Before we hung up, she said what she always does: "How can I pray for you this week?"

"Pray for my book," I said without hesitating. "I'm just beginning my chapter about money."

"That's funny," she said. "I need prayer about money, too. But it's not the money chapter in a book. It's the money chapter in our lives!" Margaret proceeded to describe the stress she and her husband have been under since they moved to a new and bigger house.

"We really thought this was the right move for us when we made it. But everything has cost so much more than we ever dreamed. Now, with the house and the kids' schools, we're getting deeper in debt every month. We prayed about our decision to buy. But now I'm just not sure whether the answer we heard was from God or from that little voice out there that's always saying, "Bigger! Better! More!"

A Monster Called More

Most of us these days are all too familiar with that little voice. We hear it calling to us from television, radio, newspapers, magazines, bulk-mail promos, billboards, and now from an army of telemarketing salespeople who have been hired to make their sales pitches during the dinner hour. We may even hear that little voice when we see our neighbor's new van or admire our friend's newly decorated den.

Author Bill Hybels has given that voice a persona and that persona a name; he's dubbed it "the monster called More."[2] Monster More is loose and on a rampage in our culture, putting a strain on everything from our pocketbooks to our marriages. How does he do it? By creating dissatisfaction with our present circumstances and erecting unrealistic expectations within our value systems. By telling us we "owe it to ourselves." By convincing us that a luxury item is a necessity and that a luxury option is standard equipment. And by numbing us to the appalling fact that the United States has 6 percent of the world's population but is daily involved in consuming 33 percent of the world's resources.[3]

The monster called More has plastered our bumpers with stickers and our T-shirts with slogans: "The One with the Most Toys Wins," "A Woman's Place Is in the

Mall," and "Put It on the Plastic." He has also managed to make shopping, charging, acquiring, and consuming a national sport. Senior citizens spend their free time "malling"—meeting friends at the mall for a little light, recreational shopping. Groups of teens roam shopping centers with discretionary money to spend. Toddlers pester parents for whatever product is most hotly promoted during Saturday morning cartoons.

This persuasive little monster has us spending our precious hours washing, dusting, shining, sorting, stacking, and storing the stuff we already own while we are building additional closets, shelves, and cabinets to make room for more. He has us buying what we don't need with money we don't have, paying for yesterday's purchases with tomorrow's paycheck, and working overtime to acquire whatever is "new," "improved," and "the very latest"—purchases that are already in the process of becoming obsolete. And we look up at some point to realize with a sinking feeling that we are possessed by our possessions instead of the other way around.

Patricia H. Sprinkle, author of *Women Who Do Too Much*, describes some of Monster More's handiwork like this:

> To me one of the saddest sights in contemporary America is a community of enormous houses standing empty five days a week while everybody goes to work in order to pay for the houses. On Saturdays the families clean and do yard work, and on Sunday they crash. No wonder! When an expensive, gorgeous home is the god, when do families really enjoy those homes? Are the houses worth the lifetimes that go to pay for them?[4]

Chronicles of a Fritterer

Spike and I certainly can't cast self-righteous aspersions

on Americans with a consumer mentality. We ourselves have been on close personal terms with the monster called More. We have consumed with the best of them.

In fact, we are the first to admit that we have never really been great with money. We are two "right brain" people who both made our worst grades in math. (I never could convince myself that all those little hypothetical problems we did in class would ever have anything to do with my real life.) The prospect of juggling all those little numbers in a budget seemed nothing short of dismal, so we basically avoided it.

Even discussing money is difficult for us. The first argument we ever had was about whether to pay for something with cash or on time. And from that day to this, money has been the one subject that can almost always get us on opposite sides of a dispute. We can discuss our faults, our mistakes, our prejudices, and our preferences. (He knows my pettiness, and I know his hang-ups.) We can talk about our hopes, our aspirations, and our secret dreams, and we can discuss each other's families without even a trace of conflict. We can talk about art, books, movies, and even the big no-nos of religion and politics. But let finances enter the picture, and we know we're treading on thin ice. It is our number-one source of conflict.

Spike and I have always been a lot better at earning money than at spending it wisely. We could get as far as putting the paycheck in the bank, but from that point, complications set in. We never had much success at getting the big picture, finding a financial direction, or making any kind of overall plan (which would require, of course, that we sit down and talk about the "M" word). And so, without a financial plan, drifting on a sea of sales and "special values" and "one-time offers" with only a checkbook and a raft of credit cards to keep us afloat, we have frittered our way through a lot of our resources.

I once heard Kris Kristofferson in concert sing his song, "Why Me?" As I remember, one of the key lines in the song is "Lord help me, Jesus, I've wasted it all." Though I've never had the big bucks of an entertainment superstar like Kristofferson, I could relate. I even considered borrowing my own version of his line—"Lord help me, Jesus, I've frittered it all."

Help for the Fritterer

I'll tell you something you may not know. There *is* help for the fritterer. There *is* help for the couple who can't seem to have a rational discussion about finances. There *is* help for anyone who has struggled with money and how to handle it and for anyone who has longed for simple, sensible ways of doing what sometimes seems "undoable"—bringing peace and order into the unruly realm of personal and family finance.

The first time I heard of Crown Ministries, my friend Pam and I were having lunch. When she mentioned that she was taking a course on money management, I almost yawned in her face. What could be less exciting?

But the more Pam talked, the more interested I became. This was a small group that met in a home. It was made up of about a dozen people who were studying a prepared series of lessons that focused on biblical principles for dealing with money. The group not only studied together, but also had a good time together. They checked on each other during the week. They helped each other and prayed for each other.

As I listened to Pam's description, I remember thinking that perhaps in a congenial group of people, all of whom were dealing with the same issues, I wouldn't be so intimidated about money. Maybe I could actually stay focused on this subject that had always managed to elude me. Maybe I could even learn something.

"Okay, so I'm curious," I finally admitted. "Tell me where to sign up."

Spike and I checked into Crown Ministries and found that it is a nonprofit Christian ministry whose twelve-week course is designed to help families simplify their finances. Crown, like other Christian financial courses such as Larry Burkett's and Ron Blue's, is designed to help us tune out the voice of Monster More and tune in to another voice instead: the voice of God.[5]

We were assigned to a Monday night small group with ten other people—some couples and some singles. That very first meeting, I remember hoping that we wouldn't be a "test case" for this ministry. (You know: "If they can help *us*, they can help anybody.") I soon found out that there were lots of different financial profiles in our group. Several folks were having big money problems. Some had no problems at all; they merely wanted to learn some better ways of dealing with their finances. Almost immediately, I stopped feeling like a test case and began to feel accepted and at home.

What we got out of the course was both practical and spiritual, both general and personal. We learned a lot of simple, practical ways to deal with money. We worked through exercises on goal setting, planning, and budgeting, and we discussed strategies for becoming debt free. But we also learned spiritual motivations for making some of these practical changes. And as we did, we found that agreeing on the "whys" made the "whats" a lot less difficult to deal with.

The results? When we started the course, Spike and I had no overall plan and a drawer full of small, unrelated debts. Today we have goals and a budget, and we are working on getting and staying debt free. Admittedly our plan is still (very much) in the experimental stages. We're still adjusting figures and learning how to monitor our old habits. But now, finally, we do have a plan. What's more, it's a plan that Spike and I worked out by sitting down together and talking about the "M" word—without killing each other! In my book, burning bushes pale by comparison to that miracle.

A Fact of Life

One personal difference that Crown has made in my life is that I no longer tiptoe around the "M" word. I'm not afraid of it anymore. Money is just a fact of life that I am finally learning to deal with. It's something that I use. And depending on how I use it, it can add harmony or confusion to my life.

Even Jesus had to deal with money. He needed it just like the rest of us to pay bills (Luke 8:1-3) and taxes (Matthew 17:24,25). I have to admit that before taking the course I never thought about Jesus having bills or paying taxes. I guess I thought he was above that. More to the point, I guess I thought *I* was above it! That's why I never really took the time to develop any kind of skill at handling money. And I suppose that's why I never bothered to see what the Bible had to say about it.

But God is certainly not too lofty to address such down-to-earth matters as money. In fact, money would appear to be one of his favorite subjects. It is mentioned in 2300 verses of the Bible, as compared to prayer, which is mentioned in only 500 verses, and faith, which is mentioned in fewer than 500.[6]

Why did God have so much to say about money? I think it was because he knew what a source of confusion and conflict it could be. He also understood what many of us have found out—that money can very quickly move into the position of a rival god in our lives. He understood that unless we learn how to keep it in its place, money can be more of a foe than a friend to us, and so he gave us some simple but radical guidelines for dealing with it.

Richard Foster, in his book *Celebration of Discipline*, spells out the central principle of financial simplicity:

The central point for the Discipline of simplicity is to seek the kingdom of God and the righteousness of his kingdom *first* and then everything necessary [including money] will come in its proper order. It is impossible to overestimate the importance of Jesus' insight on this point. Everything hinges upon maintaining the "first" thing as first.[7]

God knows we need money. He understands how important it is. But his provision of the money that he knows we need is much more likely to flow to us when we have put him and his kingdom first and put money in its place.

Life Is a Loaner

Learning to look at money from the "first things first" perspective of God's kingdom turns many of our old ideas upside-down. We don't have to dig very deep to see that "the American way" and "the kingdom way" diverge on some major points, and it may take some adjustment to get our way of thinking aligned with God's.

One of the main adjustments I have had to make in my financial outlook has to do with ownership. Like most people, I had always talked about "our house" and "our car." Spike and I had even begun to refer to "your money" and "my money." But the fact is, from God's perspective, I don't own anything. He owns it all. "To the Lord your God belong... the earth and everything in it," says the book of Deuteronomy (10:14), and the psalmist hastens to agree in Psalm 24:1 that "the earth is the Lord's, and everything in it."

Even my very life is not my own. It is a "loaner," just like the car our dealership lets us drive while our car is in the shop. We can drive the loaner, but only so long as they say so. The dealership holds the papers on it; we don't. They even carry special insurance to cover any accidents that may occur while we are driving it.

The same thing is true of my life. God is the one who owns it, and he's just letting me "drive" it for him for awhile. Everything else in my life is a loaner, too: house, car, money, everything. Even if I worked very hard for these things, they are still on loan from God. My job is a loaner; my health, my talent, and my ability to earn a living—all loaners! I can't boast about any of them: "Who says that you are better than others? Everything you have was given to you. And if this is so, why do you brag as if you got these things by your own power?" (1 Corinthians 4:7 EB).

Joyful Unconcern

The simple life is always "a life of joyful unconcern for possessions."[8] And this joyful unconcern only becomes possible when we relinquish whatever ownership rights we may have once believed we had. When we truly acknowledge God's ownership of everything in our lives, anxiety is suddenly gone. Why worry or fret or be anxious over things that are not even ours?

Our son Curt demonstrated this joyful unconcern to us last summer when his truck was broadsided and demolished just before he was to leave for Bible school in Montana. Instead of giving in to panic or despair (which would have been my tendency), he simply stated, "It's God's truck, and he knows what he's doing with it."

It was not too long before we saw what God was up to—and we were amazed. The insurance company settled on the ancient Toyota relic with an amount that was more than three times what Curt could have sold it for. The insurance money covered his remaining school tuition (something he had been praying for) and also bought three round-trip plane tickets. That settlement not only provided Curt with basic transportation to and from his school in Montana, but also enabled him to get home on Christmas and Easter in speed and comfort, without worrying about his truck "dying" on the way!

Learning to Share

Something else begins to happen as we grow to acknowledge God's ownership and our "loanership" of our lives and possessions. Eventually we begin to ask, "Lord, how would you have me share this gift? What would you have me do with *your* money . . . *your* possessions . . . *your* home?" And once we've asked, we can be sure there will be an answer. Our Father has so many children in so many parts of this planet who are in need, and one of the ways he would like to provide for them is through the gifts and money he has put in our care.

One early morning I got an SOS call from one of my prayer partners. She asked me if I would be willing to get together a box of clothes for a young woman who had fled from her abusive marriage without taking any of her own things. Picking through my closet, sensibly selecting the older garments and the things I was tired of, I was suddenly struck by the fact that every one of the dresses and skirts and blouses in my closet was nothing more than a loaner. None of them really belonged to me. Surely I could afford to be a little more extravagant with God's stuff.

As this thought dawned on me, I slowly and deliberately reached for my nearly new pink sweater and put it in the giveaway box. And that gave me another idea. Excitedly, I opened my dresser drawer and pulled out a new nightgown (with the tags still on it) and tucked that in also.

I guess I'll never know how that young, abused wife felt as she opened the box of clothes I sent her. But I know that while I was packing the clothes that morning, I experienced a wonderful surge of freedom and joy that far surpassed any excitement I could have felt buying something new for myself.

The Moth and Rust Reality

Learning to share the possessions we've been loaned is made easier by seeing these things from a heavenly perspective—as here today and gone tomorrow. Jesus counsels us not to store up earthly treasures because they will just end up making some moth a great lunch or turning to rust in some junkyard somewhere (Matthew 6:19). Why get stuck on the stuff in our lives when it doesn't last for very long anyway?

One of the silliest songs I ever wrote was on this subject. It was entitled "Moth Teeth," and the chorus went something like this (well, actually, it went exactly like this):

> But the moth has got his teeth in it; the rust is
> gonna eat it up.
> When you're shoppin' till you're droppin',
> you got nothin' left to spend on love,
> And no matter how you slice it, in the end
> it's just a bunch of stuff,
> And the moth has got his teeth in it; the rust
> is gonna eat it up.[9]

There is no greater way to prove the "moth and rust" theory to yourself than to get out an old photo album and look at things you used to treasure. When we packed for our move to the cabin, I found one dilapidated old photo album from when Spike and I were dating and first married. There I was in one picture, vain as a peacock, in my new gray and white tattersall wool dress with the little "pillbox" hat to match.

I thought I was pretty snazzy in that outfit! But where is it today? The moths have long since digested its remains.

In another photo from the same album, Spike and I were standing in front of his beautiful, new, red Chevy Corvair. We were absolutely stuck-up about that car when we first bought it, and yet today its remnants are probably at the bottom of some scrap metal heap.

Considering the fate of that pillbox hat and that Chevy Corvair adds a lot of credence to Jesus' suggestion that we're much better off sharing the earthly stuff that God has loaned us and storing up heavenly treasures instead—the kind that "moth teeth" and junkyards can't get hold of. "For where your treasure is, there your heart will be also" (Matthew 6:20,21).

A Sharing Kind of World

Once when my four-year-old nephew Kappel was encouraged to share his toys with his sister, Lilly, he informed his mother in all seriousness, "I'm sorry, Mom. I'm just not a sharing kind of guy." But what is funny and understandable in a four-year-old is tragic and destructive as part of a grown-up value system. None of us is born wanting to share, but it is an attitude we must work hard to cultivate in ourselves and our families.

I believe that hell will be a frantic, desperate place where people are clutching what they own and grabbing for more. But heaven will be a place where our hands can no longer make greedy little fists. Instead they will hold everything loosely. They will graciously and gratefully be reaching out in a continuous gesture of sharing every gift and possession.

We could experience more of heaven on earth if we would begin now to open our fists. What a simple, sensible, lovely world it would be if less of us were involved in grabbing for the money and the "stuff," and more of us were involved in helping others get their share.

Peter Maurin described such "a sharing kind of world" in these verses from his delightful poem, "Better and Better Off":

> The world would be better off
> If people tried to become better.
> And people would become better
> If they stopped trying to become better off.
> For when everybody tries to become better off,
> nobody is better off.
> But when everybody tries to become better
> everybody is better off.
> Everybody would be rich
> if nobody tried to become richer.
> And nobody would be poor
> if everybody tried to be the poorest
> And everybody would be what he ought to be
> If everybody tried to be
> What he wants the other fellow to be.[10]

Writing a Deed

The first assignment we were given in our Crown Group really helped me come to terms with God's ownership and my loanership. We were asked to formally deed everything we owned to God. Using an official-looking "quit-claim deed," we filled in a detailed list of our possessions, specifically naming everything we owned and valued. I tried to list everything I owned and cared about: family-owned items such as our home and cars as well as personal possessions such as jewelry and clothes. I even listed our two dogs, Frodo and Jubilee!

Of course, writing that deed was only a formality. If God possesses everything in heaven and earth, then obviously he was already the owner of our belongings. He already knew that. I even knew it on some theoretical level. But that deed took me out of the theoretical and into the actual.

I realize now that something important happened in the spirit realm with the signing of that deed. For it was only after Spike and I had signed, sealed, and delivered, by faith, our separate deeds to God that we began to get a joint vision of the changes he wanted to make in our family. It was only as we began to see our lives as loaners that we could begin to see a simpler lifestyle as a real possibility.

The three goals that Spike and I made at that point were very simple—simple, but not easy. We purposed together 1) to get out of debt and stay there, 2) to sell our house in town and make whatever changes were necessary to move to our cabin, and 3) to downscale our lifestyle in order to be able to give more generously, live more modestly, and save more responsibly.

A Progress Report

I would love to report to you that we have met those goals easily and soared to new spiritual heights and delights on the road to financial simplicity, but that would be a lie. This new financial vision has been very difficult to keep in sight. The road to financial simplicity has not been without its roadblocks.

The main difficulty we have wrestled with has been trying to get free of debt and live that way. Until we took the financial planning course, debt had been a way of life for us, one that we had never seriously questioned. It is, after all, the American way, isn't it? Our federal government has run up such a huge tab that even the politicians are finally getting a little worried. And there is so much personal debt in this country that the average person has been described as "someone driving on a bond-financed highway, in a bank-financed car, fueled by charge-card-financed gasoline, going to purchase furniture on the installment plan to put in his savings-and-loan financed home!"[11]

For us, learning to live debt free has been a little like withdrawing from a serious drug addiction. We did pretty well until we needed something that we didn't have the cash for. Then our banker was so willing and our credit cards were so available that we found ourselves thinking, "Aw, what's it gonna hurt? We can stop anytime we want to."

The truth is, if I wasn't totally convinced that God counsels us not to live on credit, I would have given up the struggle by now. But I'm hanging in there. We're hanging in there.

The Real Issue

The way I see it, the real issue involved in debt-free living is contentment—or, in my case, the lack of it. It's so easy for me to convince myself that some purchase or another is essential to my happiness or well-being, and if I can't have it now, I feel restless and discontent. That's when I'm tempted to reach for the plastic.

What has really helped me at this point is to realize that contentment is a learned behavior. Even the apostle Paul wrote:

> I have *learned* to be content whatever the circumstances. I know what it is to be in need, and I know what it is to have plenty. I have *learned* the secret of being content in any and every situation, whether well fed or hungry, whether living in plenty or in want. I can do everything through him who gives me strength (Philippians 4:11-13).

Money, Malls, and Moth Teeth

Paul probably wrote those words with chains on his wrists, which is a pretty awesome thought. But it encourages me to realize that he didn't just come into the world equipped with a natural flow of contentment in his personality. What he is saying here is that he has *learned* contentment. And so can I—with God's help.

Tracing the Journey

It's funny to me now, tracing my journey toward financial simplicity, to realize that the things I was lacking in the realm of finance were not mathematical skills at all. The things I have been learning that are making my life financially simpler are actually spiritual attitudes: surrender, stewardship, discipline, and contentment. Adding and subtracting are the least of it!

The farther we go on this journey toward a simpler financial life, the more people we become aware of who are moving in the same direction. It seems that everywhere I turn I am seeing magazine articles, newspaper stories, and TV news clips about people who are choosing to chart a financial course that diverges from the national consumer mindset. It seems that many of us, in our individual ways, are fighting back—turning off the television commercials and cutting up the credit cards and politely refusing to talk to the telemarketing people who phone our homes. (Actually, I'm not always that polite about it!) We are refusing to let our lives be defined by our addresses or our automobiles or the brand name on our blue jeans. We are using more of our financial resources to make a difference in the lives of others.

There is a tremendous feeling of liberation that accompanies decisions like these. George MacDonald once said that "to have what we want is riches, but to be able to do without is power."[12] I don't think I would even have understood what he was talking about a couple of years ago, but I do now. He's talking about the power of admitting that God is in control, the power of giving away what was never really ours in the first place, and the power of having a contented heart.

7
The Uncluttered Career

[The Amish] had shown me that any type of work can be meaningful. It's the spirit in which you do it that makes the difference.

—Sue Bender

❧

Our neighbor, Virgil Kelly, makes porch swings out of fallen juniper trees that he rescues from the river. Many a morning we'll hear his small motorboat putting past our cabin before we're even up, and we'll know that Virgil is out hunting wood. Later in the day we'll see him heading home again downriver, towing his prize—a massive tree trunk that he will later have milled at a little lumber mill just up the highway.

Virgil works slowly, deliberately, one swing at a time, completing just enough swings to fill the orders that trickle in, in ones and twos, from around the county. And he does good work. We can testify to that as we swing back and forth on our front porch in the evenings, comfortably cradled in one of Virgil's creations.

Virgil is in his mid-seventies now and long retired

(from the Navy, I think). He lives very simply with his wife, Annie V., in a small cement-block house just around the bend in the river. And Virgil doesn't seem to have any job stress. I would be surprised if he even knew the meaning of the term. He plies his craft with care, from gathering the supplies to turning the final screw on the finished product. Then he can look with satisfaction at the completed porch swing, the visible and tangible fruit of his labors, and enjoy the feeling of a job well done.

There is no ambiguity in a job like Virgil's. He knows why he does what he does. He makes porch swings because people want his swings, and because he needs the money, and because he likes doing work that suits his skills and talents.

A Word for the Majority

If every job were as simple and straightforward and as suited to the temperament of the worker as Virgil's is, there would be no such thing as job-related stress or professional burnout. A lot of career counselors would be out of work, and a lot of psychotherapists would find themselves with lighter workloads.

Maybe your work, like Virgil Kelly's, moves at a sane, serene, and measured pace, paying you just what you require for doing just what you enjoy. Maybe you feel comfortable and satisfied and fulfilled with what you do and the hours you spend doing it and the amount you are paid by the people who need your services. Maybe you, like Virgil, can gaze proudly at your finished product and feel the sweet peace of a job well done. If so, I might as well tell you now, this chapter is not likely to mean a whole lot to you. If you're that contented with your job situation, then you should probably write your own chapter—or at least skip reading this one.

And now, if you are still with me, let me assure you

that you are among the majority. Very few careers are as free of complications as Virgil's. Very few are as simple and logical and fulfilling. Most of us, whether we are song-writers or homemakers or nuclear physicists, struggle with complexities and ambiguities and stresses in the workplace.

My sister, Ann, for instance, who is vice president of a large Washington, D.C. public-interest lobby, must carry just a tad more career stress than Virgil Kelly does. She and Virgil probably get to work at about the same hour of the day, but there the similarity ends. While Virgil makes porch swings on an Alabama riverbank, Ann is busy juggling the varied stresses of a high-tension job in a big-city setting. She researches issues, helps write bills, handles media interviews, and often testifies before Congress. She appears on the *MacNeil-Lehrer Report* and is quoted in *The Washington Post*, and last year she taught a course at Harvard as part of their guest lecture series. I feel stressed just talking to her on the telephone!

To add to her already hectic load, this year Ann has decided to finish the requirements for an advanced degree, and this extra effort has pretty much put her over the edge. She has always loved her job, but now she finds herself exhausted and depleted and very close to burnout. In fact, she confided to her friend Randy the other day that she was considering going into a new field.

"Oh yeah? And what's that?" Randy wanted to know.

"I was watching this special on Mother Teresa last night, and she seems so serene and fulfilled," Ann said. "So I was thinking maybe I could be a Saint—the kind with a capital letter."

"I hate to tell you, Ann," Randy quipped, "but that is not a career move."

Work and Worship

Maybe Randy's right, but there *is* something irresistible about Mother Teresa. I look into her weatherbeaten old face, so heavily lined by a million compassionate smiles and a million expressions of concern, and I am forced to rethink my definition of beauty. Here is beauty you cannot get out of a jar of face cream. Here is beauty that radiates from the deep fires of faith that are banked within.

But we would be wrong to think that Mother Teresa's daily life is free of complication. Quite the contrary. In fact, her job description would read a lot more like my sister Ann's than Virgil Kelly's. Mother Teresa's job is anything but simple. The tasks she takes on and the work she accomplishes in a week would exhaust a woman half her age. She travels and speaks before groups. She meets with and instructs the nuns and novices in her order. She makes decisions regarding the running of the hospitals and homes in her care. She visits and cares for the patients and residents of these charitable institutions, bringing them hope and courage. She takes time out to meet with the many visitors who come to Calcutta to see her and observe her ministry, invariably inviting them to join with her in the work. She also prays . . . and prays.

And yet, even knowing how full of complications workdays can be, when I see her face on a TV special or read about her life in an article or a book, I am invariably struck by the simplicity and serenity that seem to go right down to the core of who she is. There is something about the way she "lives and moves and has her being" that seems to hold her above the confusion and distress of ordinary life.

Our friend Gerrit Gustaffson, who travels the world teaching on the subject of worship, got a clue to Mother Teresa's serene simplicity when he had the opportunity to meet with her several years ago in Calcutta. In their brief meeting, he spoke to her about the worldwide explosion of worship music that he is so excited about. But the more he talked, the more he realized that she had little understanding of or interest in the subject of worship music.

Finally, realizing he was not getting through, Gerrit asked Mother Teresa a very simple question: "What does worship mean to you?" He was touched and challenged by her answer, which richly enhanced his own ideas about worship.

"We worship God by living out our lives before him," she answered, "by going out and finding the poorest of the poor and then taking care of them. This is what gives God glory."

Mother Teresa is definitely one of those "elemental" souls whose life is all of a piece, whose daily occupation is so in sync with her deepest beliefs that she finds no *distinction between her work and her worship.*

Nitty-Gritty Remedies for Everyday Realities

Very few of us have jobs in which our work and our worship are interchangeable. Some of us even have jobs that sometimes seem to butt heads with what we value most. And probably many of us have days when we would love to run away from the complexity and routine of our jobs and instead do something very simple, like building porch swings on a riverbank, or something deeply fulfilling, like ministering to the dying on the streets of Calcutta.

But these, most likely, are only daydreams, not real-life considerations. And most of us, I imagine, would warmly welcome some truly practical advice on how to make our real-life workdays more sane and simple. We could use some nitty-gritty ideas on how to reduce our stress and increase our sense of satisfaction on the job, how to bring more serenity into an arena that can feel like pure turmoil, and how to create more unity between what we believe and what we do.

Most of the ideas that I've gleaned and gathered on this subject of how to "unclutter a career" have come from talking to people whom I admire. In fact, I have found this topic to be a wonderful conversation starter everywhere I've gone for the past few weeks. Almost every working person I've talked to has struggled to find ways of making his or her work simpler and more satisfying.

I have spoken to professional people and part-time workers, to people who go to work in office buildings and people who work in their homes, to people in "left brain" cognitive careers and to "right brain" artist types. And I have been amazed and delighted to find so much wisdom and creativity, so many well-thought-out, articulately expressed ideas on simplicity to supplement the ideas and information I have found in books and discovered for myself. I have grouped and blended and combined all of these ideas and come up with a dozen useful principles, which I am happy to share with you here.

They may not turn us into Mother Teresa. They may not turn our stress-filled jobs into Virgil Kelly jobs. But if even one of these ideas helps you begin to simplify the way you work, I will be happy, and you will be ahead of the game. So without further ado, here they are.

A Dozen Dandy, Stress-Stripping, Simplicity-Inducing Principles for You to Take to Work

🌳 Ask Advice from People You Admire

I start with this principle for an obvious reason: My informal inquiry into different people's methods for simplifying their jobs has yielded a bumper crop of ideas. In fact, I've learned so much that now I wonder why I never asked before. Was it was laziness or stubbornness or pride?

The book of Proverbs counsels us over and over again to seek wise counsel in all our affairs:

> Listen to advice and accept instruction, and in the end you will be wise (Proverbs 19:20).

> The way of a fool is right in his own eyes, but a wise man is he who listens to counsel (Proverbs 12:15 NASB).

> The wise man is glad to be instructed, but a self-sufficient fool falls flat on his face (Proverbs 10:8 TLB).

If there is someone you observe at work every day who seems to be "living, moving, and having her being" in a place called Simplicity, by all means approach that person and ask her how she does it! If you have a parent or a relative or a friend who seems to possess the gift of doing his job with a sense of efficiency and calm, don't be shy. Confess your longing to work in more simple and satisfying ways and pick that person's brain. Most people will be flattered that you want their advice and will be all too willing to share what they know.

❦ Get the Big Picture

One of the things that impressed me most on my first visit to Word Music Publishers in Nashville was their large, beautifully calligraphied, handsomely framed Mission Statement. I don't even remember what it said exactly; I just remember being struck with the fact that they had taken the time to sum up who they were, have it written on one ivory-colored piece of parchment, frame it, and hang it on the wall.

That is what I mean by getting the big picture. It is stepping back from the job and trying to paint it in broad strokes. It is making an effort to think through what you are doing each day and why, as well as what good is served by the fact that you are doing it.

An elementary-school teacher, for example, might write a mission statement that goes something like this:

> I am helping to shape the minds and hearts and consciences of thirty-one eight-year-olds by giving them my time and attention every day. I am investing my best creative efforts into the planning and presenting of my lesson plans. I am teaching wholesome values and modeling a balanced lifestyle. I am trying to see each child as a unique and valuable individual and helping each one become the best person he or she can be.

On days when this teacher is overwhelmed by hordes of wiggling third graders—and stacks of their test papers, and oceans of lunch-money reports and attendance records—she can reread her mission statement and remember what her job is really all about.

Many of the people I interviewed who had had some success at simplifying their work lives had spent time thinking about and writing down some kind of a personal mission statement. Maybe they didn't call it that. Some people called it a job description; others called it a list of goals and priorities. But whatever they called it, the document they put together was an overview of their work and what they hoped to accomplish, stated in the most compelling language they could come up with. And it did the job of helping them look beyond the tedious little tasks they had to perform each day and remember why they are doing the job in the first place.

All of us were born gifted; we are naturally good at something. Maybe you are naturally graceful or naturally good at math or naturally gifted at putting colors together. Whenever you can manage to involve your natural gifts in doing a job, the job feels easier, it goes more smoothly, and the finished product is usually better. Nothing feels more frustrating than working day by day at a job that makes no use whatsoever of your strong points.

I simplified my songwriting career when I made the decision to "go with my gift" of lyric writing. My first several years in this profession, I wrote both lyrics *and* music, but it didn't take me long to figure out that my mediocre melodies were pulling down my strongest asset, my words. At that point, I could have decided to go back to school and start from scratch, studying composition and music theory. Instead, I chose to go with my gift by concentrating on lyrics. I began collaborating with musically gifted composers whose melodies could further strengthen my strength of writing lyrics. This decision has brought a lot of clarity and simplicity to my career. I have never regretted making it.

Ideally, of course, the work we do to make our living will be work that draws on our strengths and uses our gifts. Unfortunately, that's not always possible. With a little creativity, however, I think we can make our work simpler by finding ways to use our gifts effectively in our work.

My brother, Charlie, for example, is a gifted poet who has had many individual poems published in literary journals and even had a book published,[1] but he butters his family's bread by working every day for a large corporation. A right-brain poet would seem to be something of a misfit in the corporate world, especially since he is working for a company that hires mostly engineers. But Charlie has found a way to get paid for doing work that he is good at, thereby maximizing his effectiveness to his company and his own enjoyment of the work.

He has made the company newsletter, of which he is editor, publisher, and chief reporter, a polished and attractive publication. He has also researched, written, and published a quality-control manual for his employer. Using an in-house employee to do these specialized jobs has saved Charlie's company money and has also given him an opportunity to use his gift of writing, thereby making his work more pleasurable.

Finding more ways to go with your gifts at work can simplify your life tremendously. But how do you determine what your gifts are? Your interest and energy level are clues to what your gifts might be. What tasks tend to capture your imagination or get you excited instead of draining you? Do you love to reorganize the file cabinets? Do you shine at meetings or thrive on troubleshooting snags in the workflow? Follow those clues. Perhaps your job description can be tweaked to put your gifts to better use. Or at very least, you can begin setting some long-term goals for landing a job that helps you go with your gifts.

❦ Ask Yourself the Right Questions

Most people who are trying to simplify their lives have developed the habit of dialoguing with their "better judgment." This can be a very helpful process if you are asking yourself the right questions! Here are some of the most helpful "simplifying questions" I have been able to glean from the working people I interviewed:

"How important is this task really? Is this something I could delegate or eliminate?" Ellen, a newspaper editor, asked herself, "How important are all these beautifully typed letters I'm churning out each day?" Ellen now eliminates much of her correspondence by scrawling a

one-sentence handwritten answer in the margins of letters of inquiry she receives. She then pops the original letter, with her answer on it, into an envelope and sends it right back to its sender. The person receiving Ellen's answer has the benefit of having in hand not only her brief, written (and prompt) reply but also his own inquiry in case he needs to review it.

Michelle, a full-time homemaker and mother of four, has learned to ask similar questions about her daily work. She considers the children to be her main priority, and to do a good job of tending to their needs she has had to relegate a lot of household tasks to bottom priority. Fuss-budget neatness has no place in Michelle's work ethic. Laundry, meals, and a basic semblance of order suffice on a daily level. Big jobs like cleaning the oven and washing the windows are tackled infrequently. And how important are the little chores of the compulsively clean—like dusting baseboards and polishing doorknobs? Not very! They have all but been eliminated from Michelle's routine for the time being.

By asking himself the "how important" question, my brother, Johnny, a plaintiff's attorney, has made the difficult but freeing decision to begin limiting his individual caseload, even though doing so may mean a drop in yearly income. But how important is it to "grow" a practice that devours your entire life? Johnny has decided that it's better to limit your work than to have your work limit your life!

"Can I work simpler?" Sylvia, a teacher, spends an hour or two on Sunday evenings reviewing the coming week at school and anticipating the complications that could arise. By constantly thinking creatively and searching for simpler ways to work with her pupils, she is able to make her job less chaotic. Sylvia actually jots down her ideas for simplifying each area of potential confusion, such as making transitions between subjects or

executing complicated projects in the classroom. Here are some examples:

- Between reading and math, have children put their heads on their desks until all members of the reading groups have returned to their places.

- Ask volunteers to stay in during break to help me prepare papier maché materials for art class. Have everything ready when children come in.

- Appoint team leaders to line up groups of ten when coming back from library. Give points to the quietest team and allow the team with the most points to go to the cafeteria first.

Sylvia has found that time spent thinking through these knotty problems at home saves time and confusion with the children in the classroom. This technique could be successfully adapted to other professions that tend toward complexity and confusion.

"How does this task fit in with my life goals?" My songwriter friend Nancy was able to simplify her workload considerably by asking herself whether teaching piano lessons was really contributing to her overall writing goals. The extra money from the lessons was helpful. But Nancy decided that giving up her piano students would be a wise financial decision in the long run because it would allow her more time and energy to concentrate on her primary goal of songwriting.

"What would Jesus do?" Roland, a counselor in an adolescent chemical-dependency program in a hospital, deals with a lot of confusion and stress in his very demanding job. He has discovered that the question which

brings immediate clarity to almost any problem is, "What would Jesus do in this situation?" Roland finds that allowing Jesus' wisdom and viewpoint and especially his Holy Spirit to work in stressful situations is the surest path to serenity and simplicity.

🐝 Build in Rewards

If your particular job situation leaves you short on affirmation and rewards—either because your boss isn't the affirming type or because you don't have a boss—try not to let the lack of "strokes" be a source of stress. You can join your own fan club and bring some encouragement into your work day by "building in" some rewards for yourself for a job well done. For example:

- Buy a special bath oil or bubble bath to use when you get home after an extra hard day at the office.

- When you close a deal or finish an assignment, send yourself a single rose.

- Take a "serenity lunch break" after a stressful morning. Carry a sandwich and a book of poems or meditations to a nearby park. Dwelling on something lovely and inspiring right in the middle of the day can renew your spirit and bring you the encouragement you need.

- Look for little ways to reward your co-workers when they need a boost, too.

🐝 Make Your Workplace "You"

A sense of unity and simplicity comes from being who you are wherever you are, and personalizing your physical work environment can help you do this. The extent to which you personalize depends on the job, of course—some companies seem determined to depersonalize their employees. But most people can find ways to bless themselves on the job by building a nurturing environment.

My dad has an extra-long sofa in his office that accommodates his six-foot-six frame. He finds that a fifteen-minute "refresher snooze" can revitalize him and send him back to work a new man. President John F. Kennedy, who had a bad back, kept a rocking chair in his office to give his back a restful change of position.

Interior designer Alexandra Stoddard feels more productive and creative in a visually stimulating environment, surrounded by a variety of colors and textures around her. Floral paintings of flowers on her walls, colored pencils in a jar for "doodling," and bright print boxes for storing projects give her spirits a lift and remind her of her commitment to bring color and beauty into the lives of her clients as well.[2]

Even the smallest personalizing touch can help you keep things simple on the job. For instance, a nicely framed picture of your family on your desk can remind you of your priorities. (They can also remind you to get home a little early today if possible to spend some quality moments with the people you love.) At the very least, a small satchel of "personal stuff" in your locker—a book, a photo or two, a jar of your favorite perfume—can give you a dash of perspective when you go on breaks and remind you of who you are and why you are working.

❦ Have a Strong Support System

We were not meant to go through life as "lone rangers." A strong network of caring friends can mean the difference between stress and distress on the job.

Our friend Phillip, who runs The Shoulder, a Christian drug and alcohol rehab center, knows well the meaning of the word *stress*. When I asked him what makes his complex, demanding job bearable, he didn't hesitate.

"Praying with my friend Richard every Wednesday has been the main thing that has helped me stay sane when it gets crazy. Richard knows everything about me—the good, the bad, and the ugly—and he accepts me unconditionally. But he also challenges me when I'm tired and my perceptions get a little skewed. He tells me to slow down. He helps me stay focused on my priorities. He listens when I need to talk. And he prays when I'm in a jam. He's a true friend."

Luanne, an advertising executive, attributes her serenity on the job to the Thursday noon Al Anon meeting she attends in a church basement near her office. "Most of us in the group are career women with families," she says. "We understand each other's stress. Every week the wisdom and encouragement I take away from my meeting is like a life vest that keeps me afloat till the next meeting."

Tom, an anesthesiologist, has a grueling schedule, but his wife, Lisa, tells me that the one appointment he bounds out of bed to make in the morning is his weekly breakfast with three close friends who share and pray for one another. He says he couldn't do without it.

Like Phillip, Luanne, and Tom, I find friends and spiritual support indispensable ingredients in keeping my job sane and simple. I have a special "team" of friends who are committed to praying for me and my work—my writing projects as well as my speaking schedule. I always try to let them know when I'm traveling, especially if I'm teaching or leading a retreat, so they can be holding me up in prayer.

🐚 *Learn to Enjoy the Process*

Tino, a sculptor and a poet, said that what counts

most is not the end results, but "the enjoyment of every step in the process of doing—everything, not only the isolated piece we label art. . . . If you rush to the accomplishment, it is an inevitable disappointment. Then you rush to something else [and] the disappointment is reaped over and over again. But if every step is pleasant, then the accomplishment becomes even more, because it is nourished by what is going on."[3]

When I teach a songwriting class or seminar, I am always careful to caution those aspiring to professional status in the music industry, "Writing songs must be your passion. You must love each step in the process dearly. If you are waiting for success to bring the joy, it may never come and you will have worked for nothing. But if you love the words and the process of stringing them together, if you love the notes and building each melody, then success may come quickly or slowly or never come at all, and you will still have lived a life filled with purpose and beauty and joy."

🌱 Know When to Stop

I need this advice more than anyone I know. Sometimes I will get into a writing frenzy (especially when I am under a deadline), and I can't seem to "put the period" to what I am doing. The result is almost always that I end up feeling exhausted and creatively spent. I'm also likely at such points of weariness to become my own guest at my own personal pity party. "Poor me. I never get to stop," I moan, when the truth is that I don't let myself stop—or, more importantly, *make* myself stop!

Many recovery programs recommend using a simple little acronym, H.A.L.T., to prevent a lapse into unhealthy behavior. The letters stand for the words *hungry*, *angry*, *lonely*, and *tired*. Learning to put on the breaks when one of those words applies to our lives is a way of working wisely and simply. Take a break, get a grip, meet your needs, and you'll come back to work in a much more sane and productive state of mind.

Living out here in the country, I have learned to be especially sensitive to the times that I'm lonely for a visit with a friend. I am basically an extrovert, and I know that my work will suffer if I don't take time out for friendships. Nothing is better for my perspective and my energy level than turning the computer off and getting together with a friend who makes me laugh.

🍒 Learn to Let Go

Perfectionism is the kiss of death when it comes to working simply. Perfectionism can dam up the creative flow in a work environment quicker than anything I know. As writer Melodie Beattie puts it:

> We do a terrible, annoying thing to ourselves and others when we expect perfection. We set up a situation where others, including ourselves, do not feel comfortable with us. Sometimes, expecting perfection makes people so uptight that they and we make more mistakes than normal because we are so nervous and focused on mistakes.[4]

Tim, a department manager in a large corporation, has learned to give his perfectionist expectations to God. He has learned to hold up high standards at work without demanding perfection from the people in his department. Tim says that he is finding tremendous joy in watching how much better work people do when he gives them simple affirmation and encouragement instead of putting them into a straitjacket of perfectionism.

🍒 Discover the Ministry in the Midst

Mary, a clinical therapist at a children's home, is

frequently frustrated by the long, stressful on-duty hours she puts in every week, as well as by the lack of commitment she sometimes experiences on the part of her coworkers. When her frustration is at its highest, she tries to put her focus on the "ministry in the midst of the work." That is, she tries to stop seeing her work as a job and to look at the deeper level of ministry involved instead.

It may be easier to see a children's home as a place of ministry than an ordinary office or factory. But the truth is that there are people in every workplace who need ministry—hurting people who need the encouragement and hope that comes just from knowing someone cares. Being open to this aspect of our work can be tremendously effective in bringing a sense of unity to what we do. When we manage to make ministry our focus, our lives are no longer bifurcated into the work segment and the spiritual segment.

🍎 Do the Next Thing

When the job is hectic and the confusion is closing in, remind yourself that God is in it with you, helping you to do the next thing and then the next. In fact, "it is God which worketh in you both to will and to do of his good pleasure" (Philippians 2:13 KJV).

Our friend Bradley, an attorney, experiences most of his job stress when he is facing a day of work out of town, away from his own familiar turf. Bradley finds his inner peace and greatly simplifies his workday by reading a few psalms in his hotel room the night before and then getting a good night's sleep. He wakes rested, trusting God to take him through the commitments of his day one at a time.

What better prescription for inner peace than words like these?

He who dwells in the shelter of the Most
High will rest in the shadow of the almighty
(Psalm 91:1).

He will call upon me, and I will answer him;
I will be with him in trouble, I will deliver
him and honor him (Psalm 91:15).

Find rest, O my soul, in God alone; my hope
comes from him. He alone is my rock and
my salvation; he is my fortress, I will not be
shaken (Psalm 62:5,6).

Knowing that God is there, working right in the
thick of it all, invested in our concerns and wanting us to
get through it by his grace, can be a tremendously calming and comforting thought when we are feeling frantic.
If we can just "remember to remember" this wonderful
reality, we can allow God to hold our stress and worry.
And this in turn can free us simply to "do the next thing"
. . . and then the next thing . . . and then the next. Before
we know it, the job will be done.

Very few of us will ever find ourselves, like Mother
Teresa, in the capital-letter-Saint category, where work
and worship are all of a piece. Very few of us will be
allowed the luxury of making a living in as rustic and
relaxed a career as Virgil Kelly's porch-swing enterprise.
But all of us can find ways to work more sanely and more
simply at whatever profession we have found ourselves
involved in. All of us can determine to defuse our "workaholic tendencies" and give ourselves permission to rest.
All of us can look for the ministry in the midst of what we
do. We can learn to let God hold the stress while we
simply "do the next thing."

Mother Teresa does not have the market cornered
on simplicity or serenity. If we're seeking it and staying
open to it, we will find that there is plenty to go around
in my workplace and in yours.

8

Pockets of Heaven on the Apron of Earth

*I*f I had only . . . forgotten future greatness and looked at the green things and the buildings and reached out to those around me and smelled the air and ignored the forms and the self-styled obligations and heard the rain on my roof and put my arms around my wife . . . perhaps it's not too late.

—Hugh Prather

❧

I loved Harrison Ford in the title role of the movie *Regarding Henry*. A cold and emotionless corporate attorney, Henry is the victim of a shooting accident and loses his memory. During the long, difficult recovery process, Henry has an amazing realization: He does not like the man he was before the accident. As he regains his physical and mental faculties, Henry also begins to restructure his value system. He becomes a gentle, compassionate man with an almost childlike outlook. He walks away from the drivenness of his law practice and learns the value of just being with the family he loves. For the first time in his life, he comes to understand the simple rhythm of rest.

We are a nation that has always placed a high value on the kind of man Henry was before his accident and always looked somewhat askance at the kind of man he came to be. We are not far removed from an era in which leisure has been viewed with uneasiness among the serious working class. The very idea of working less has been extremely uncomfortable for many of us. "If we worked less we would suddenly be confronted with the problem of freedom and what to do with it."[1]

Too often, work has also been our way of placing a value on ourselves. If we have logged so many hours or closed so many deals (or in my case, written so many pages) in a day, then we have earned our right to breathe the oxygen for twenty-four more hours. Even our available free time is often spent "in the most strenuous possible activity, because this means we're not doing nothing. We're not sloshing aimlessly around in the swimming pool just because it's cool and pleasant. We're swimming laps, counting as we turn."[2] We have found ourselves unable to spend an hour of unplanned leisure (resting, relaxing, or merely sitting in a chair thinking) without feeling we were somehow weird or dull or (the worst sin of all) nonproductive.

When Leisure Came Naturally

But none of us were born workaholics. Most of us as children knew how to "kick back" and have fun. It was as natural as breathing.

I grew up in a whole neighborhood of kids who really knew how to "do leisure." We spent long hours being cowboys and cowgirls (and Sylvia Martin always had to be the Indian). And then at some point the game would change and we would all be the horses instead, doing the whole game over from the animals' viewpoint. We'd play dolls for hours, and then, when we were ready for some action, we'd play army in the "forts" we had set

Pockets of Heaven on the Apron of Earth

up under the walls of the big stucco gates at the front of our subdivision.

We chose teams for games of softball and Red Rover. We produced elaborate dramas in the Burdens' backyard. And one year we had a pet show in which we invited every kid in the neighborhood to enter the animal of his choice. Dad was the honored judge who gave a prize to everyone—"Funniest Fish," for instance, or "Dog with the Shortest Legs."

Summer afternoons after lunch, cooled by the churning of a huge attic fan, we'd suck on Kool-Aid ice cubes and read Nancy Drew mysteries. Summer evenings we'd play hide-and-seek or spotlight in our yard or the Morvants' until the air was thick and electric with "lightning bugs" and we could hear our moms calling our names like verses in a familiar song, "Claire! Ann! Carolyn! Joanie! Bobby! J.J.! Jeannie! Lennie Lou! Freddy! Sylvia! Leah! Linda! Time to come in!" After a bath and a goodnight kiss, we'd fall into bed, bone weary, and drift off to sleep thinking about what we'd play tomorrow.

Looking back at those "Norman Rockwell" days has got me thinking: What a sad state we're in when what once was natural is no longer natural. How ironic that resting, relaxing, reflecting, and rejoicing should have to become learned behaviors. How tragic to have lost the ability to slow down, enter in, experience with our full feelings the wonder of nature and life and each other. And how lamentable that what once made us feel good has acquired the power to make us feel guilty.

One of my goals in moving to the country has been to relearn how to rest and recreate, to reclaim the ability to let go and enjoy my leisure and learn to feel good about times when I am not doing or achieving anything. This has not been easy for me. Strong workaholic tendencies can drive a person to work anytime, anywhere, no matter how tranquil her setting.

Pockets of Heaven on the Apron of Earth

The Rest We Need

I could take some comfort, I suppose, in knowing that I'm not alone. I am, in fact, part of a huge subculture of driven Americans, nurtured on the post-Depression work ethic, who have come to think of rest as a shameful and frivolous luxury. But rest is far from shameful or frivolous. It is, in fact, a necessity that most of us tired, busy Americans desperately need.

The rest we need however is the kind that goes deeper than a catatonic rendezvous with a nightly string of sitcoms or a driven participation in sports activities that become a mere extension of the work-week mentality! The recreation we need is the kind which actually re-creates. We need recreation that separates us for a time from consumerism, competition, and status seeking, recreation that offers more than the expensive brand of "relaxation" being peddled to us by this country's billion-dollar leisure industry.

Admit it. When you think of leisure, you probably grab your wallet or your checkbook. Just say the word *vacation* or *recreation*, and most of us immediately think in terms of plane tickets and admissions, hotels and restaurants, sports equipment and club memberships.

But real rest that re-creates cannot be purchased on the open market. Real rest is the gift we can only discover when we are finally committed to slowing down and easing up.

"If we turn down speed and noise enough to notice," says Doris Janzen Longacre, author of *Living More with Less*, "life is ready with free thrills and gifts of beauty."[3] She backs up this belief in her book by providing pages of free or inexpensive leisure activities to do with family and friends, as well as nuggets of wisdom from real people who attest to being re-created by their recreation rather than bankrupted and burned out by it.

Pockets of Heaven on the Apron of Earth

What to Do at a Log Cabin

Living here in the country, I am finding fun and beauty, rest and recreation, in the most ordinary things. Just opening my eyes to what is around me, I am discovering a world of simple and relaxing pleasures. I sometimes forget how much I've changed until I see our life here at Juniper Landing through someone else's eyes.

Not long ago, some friends from Los Angeles took the trouble to wind their van down the necessary back roads to find our cabin. I think they were truly alarmed to find us making our home in such a primitive spot.

"It's beautiful," their teenage daughter ventured nervously, "but what does a person *do* at a log cabin?" Spike and I looked at each other and laughed, realizing that there was probably no possible way we would ever convince this "Valley Girl" that there is fun to be had out here away from the fast track.

Prompted by her question, however, I have begun to realize what a wealth of simple, restful pleasures there are to enjoy here in the deepest wilds of Alabama.

For instance, blueberry and blackberry picking are among my spring and summer delights. Some mornings we just step out the back door and gather enough berries from our own bushes or vines to garnish our cereal bowls. When our friends or our children come out from town during berry season, we equip them with bags and baskets and go on real "berry quests." What a wonderful setting for idle chatter among kindred spirits! And we always come home with the added bonus of baskets filled with ingredients for cobbler and homemade ice cream!

Ken and Renee Johannsan, our neighbors up the road, have expanded on the theme of berry picking with an annual party they call "The Blueberry Open Frisbee Golf Tournament." People arrive with children, guitars, Frisbees, and baskets for picking. We try not to miss the event each year.

Gathering wildflowers and arranging them is another therapeutic and restful way to spend time here at Juniper Landing. Stargazing is yet another. Lying in the dark on a quilt and looking up into a million diamond lights is a quiet and rejuvenating pastime—one that is available to many town-dwellers as well.

One of Spike's favorite leisure activities is to turn up his Pavarotti opera tapes loud enough to be heard from the river, especially just at sunset. Then he'll drift in a canoe or an inner tube and have a multimedia show, watching the sun set and listening to that glorious tenor voice echo out across the water.

(One late afternoon he was indulging in this simple pleasure, unaware that a local fisherman was casting for bass in some weeds near our shoreline. "What kind of music is that?" the fisherman asked loudly and abruptly, startling Spike. But Spike quickly regained his composure. "That's Garth Brooks singing Italian," Spike quipped. I don't think the fisherman was fooled!)

"Critter watching" is another restful country pleasure we don't take for granted. This year we watched baby wrens hatching in a window box just outside our bedroom window. Raccoons, rabbits, deer, possums, and wild turkey are frequent guests at our little domain. In the past few weeks, an osprey has taken to observing our cabin about five o'clock every afternoon from the branch of a tree just across the river. And one morning, when I was talking on the portable phone on the river porch, I suddenly threw the phone down and began whooping with delight. Spike came running to see what the commotion was. And there, swimming past the cabin were two porpoises that managed to make their way up river from the bay. (When I say our home is like a zoo, it's more than a figure of speech!)

Other rest-inducing brands of recreation we enjoy are napping on the rainy afternoon, gathering driftwood, making vine wreaths, and reading books aloud to one

Pockets of Heaven on the Apron of Earth

another. But perhaps the most enjoyable pastime for me at Juniper Landing is good dinner-table conversation when guests come out from town. Something about this laid-back country setting seems to oil the wheels of communication.

Our friend Mallie has invented a wonderful way of shifting dinner-table conversation from light chatting to real sharing. Turning her dinner knife upside-down and using the handle of it for a microphone, she poses a candid question to whatever group is gathered, asking each person to answer into the "mike" as it is passed. We've been using "Mallie's Microphone Method" for table talk here at the Landing with great results. Here are some of the questions that have sparked wonderful rounds of talk at our table:

- What was the hardest thing you had to go through this past year?

- What is the dumbest thing you ever did?

- If you could say "thank you" to one person in your life, who would it be, and what would you thank him or her for?

Rest Is a State of Mind

These are just a sampling of some of the simple, satisfying, sometimes silly ways we rest and recreate here in the country. But this is a vital point: You don't have to live rural to learn to rest in simple ways!

Most big cities, for instance, are packed with things to do, many of them free or inexpensive. When we visit my sister in Washington, D.C., for instance, we are thrilled by the many forms of relaxation that are available to us, from strolling through museums to gawking at historical monuments to stopping at beautiful old churches where we can steal a quiet moment in the midst of all the rush

Pockets of Heaven on the Apron of Earth

and noise. And years ago, when we lived in New Orleans, I would walk to the corner with baby Curt in tow and ride a streetcar just to get away for awhile. I loved watching the people and taking in the sights, and Curt usually slept soundly in my arms to the rock and the rattle of the ride.

Every small town also has its own unique set of simple, noncompetitive, restful pleasures to be discovered and enjoyed: picnics, parades, local customs and crafts. Within thirty minutes of our cabin, dozens of small-town festivals offer a cornucopia of local color, fun, food, music, and "arts and crafts" to area residents and visitors. Some of our favorites are the Elberta German Sausage Festival, the Fairhope Arts and Crafts Show, and the Blakely Bluegrass Music Festival.

Rest is truly not a function of where you live. It is a matter of shifting the way you think and allowing yourself to relax into the moment. So many forms of simple rest and recreation are available to almost anybody living almost anywhere: family time, evenings with friends, good books, playgrounds, romps with the dog, hobbies and crafts.

We can teach our children valuable lessons in resourcefulness and appreciation by including them in our pursuit of restful recreation. Our two sons grew up watching us make music with our friends and family members. Dinner guests often arrived with their guitars, basses, autoharps, or banjos, and after dinner we would provide our own easygoing entertainment. Now we see our adult children, both accomplished guitarists themselves, sharing the simple pleasure of making music with their own friends.

John Hadamuscin, in his little book, *Simple Pleasures*, recalls with gratitude the encouragement his parents gave him to enjoy simple forms of recreation:

> From the time we were small kids, my parents encouraged my brothers, my sister and

Pockets of Heaven on the Apron of Earth

me to take pleasure in those sweet and simple moments that can pop up on any old day, those moments that are sometimes spontaneous, and never over orchestrated. As I've gotten older, and life continues to become more complicated and complex, I suppose I'm just like everyone else—those simple things, those simple pleasures, continue to be what often make me most happy.[4]

God's Rhythm of Rest

Simple pleasures that are connected with real rest and recreation do much more for us than merely "make us happy." They also make us whole.

This kind of rest meets a fundamental requirement within the human personality. The fact is, we were created with a need for it. The basic instructions for "the care and feeding of the human being" list rest as an essential maintenance tool. Taking time off to "keep Sabbath" was one of God's top ten priorities for the well-being of his creation (see Leviticus 25:1-7; Deuteronomy 15:1-11). For Christians, it is a spiritual imperative.

One of the Scripture paraphrases in my book, *Postcards from Heaven*, states the Lord's heavenly admonition to rest like this (it is based on Isaiah 58:13,14 and Exodus 20:8-11):

> Dear child of mine,
>
> Has it ever occurred to you that even I rested on the seventh day! Do you think I was tired? The God of all power and might? The God of unfathomable strength? No, I rested on the seventh day so that you would see and understand that rest is part of the rhythm of my creation. It is woven into the fabric of my plan. It is my commandment for you.

Turn your heart toward me and delight in my Sabbath. If you honor me by ceasing from your own drivenness, by turning away from your own restless pursuits to spend time with me, you will discover my joy.

Rest in me,

God[5]

When exhausted people moan, "Stop the world, I wanna get off," they are demonstrating their basic, God-given, inner need for rest and recreation. When the springs of our world are so tightly wound that we feel we are ready to come out of our skin like a jack out of his box, we require God's rhythm of rest to unwind emotionally and spiritually.

A story I read recently underscored how essential our need for rest is. It seems that some African missionaries had hired a number of native workers to carry their supplies from one village to another. The missionaries, possessed of the American "push-rush-hurry" mentality, verbally prodded their native employees every day to go a little faster and a little farther than they had the day before. Finally, after three days of being pushed and hurried, the native workers sat down and refused to move.

"What in the world is the problem?" the American missionaries wanted to know. "We have been making excellent time. There's no need to stop here."

"It is not wise to go so rapidly," the spokesman for the native workers explained. "We have moved too fast yesterday. Now today we must stop and wait here for our souls to catch up with our bodies!"[6]

Without knowing it, this African worker was explaining the biblical perspective on rest to a missionary who should have known it. God has woven a beautiful silver strand of rest into the fabric of his plan for our lives. When the world we live in prods and pushes us to follow its hectic pace, we need to take time to rediscover the healing pattern of God's plan. We must embrace his rhythm of rest so that our souls will have a chance to catch up with our bodies.

A Sabbath Cease-Fire

My husband has always been a hard worker, but he has always been good at letting his soul keep pace with his body. He is what I would call a world-class "rester." His understanding of Sabbath restoration is far broader than the confines of Sunday worship, for he sees Sabbath as any time set apart for healing rest. He sees it as a time of getting in touch with God and his wonders and allowing them to restore us to wholeness. This kind of Sabbath can happen on a Saturday morning or a Tuesday afternoon or whenever we make a space for it.

Spike's journal is full of his insightful Sabbath experiences. Here's just a sampling from his "Juniper Journal":

A large grackle lands on a vine, almost within arm's reach, and studies me intently, cocking its head from side to side, peering at me first from one golden eye and then the other. As I slowly raise my camera this bird leaps with such a start that an autumn-browned leaf is knocked loose by its wing beat and the bird is out of sight before the loosened leaf lands upon my shoe. . . . I do love this place so. I feel the immediate presence of God in this October swamp. I think of it as a place that he has mostly completed, and that he looks in on from time to time, nodding and chuckling to himself as to its subtle perfection. Surely today, this very

147

day in October, he is passing through— perhaps as Grackle Companion. I am much blessed to have been here, too. I have had his leaf on my shoe.[7]

When we are willing to halt and declare a Sabbath in our lives, we are meeting one of our most essential needs. When we call a cease-fire on the nine-to-five battlefront, we are giving God permission to fly his flag of peace over our lives. We are giving our spirits a chance to put things into perspective. When we stop and rest in him, our ambitions are tamed, our anxieties are soothed, our earthly cares are shrunk to their actual size, and we are healed in mysterious ways that only God can fully understand. As Wendell Berry so eloquently put it:

> The mind that comes to rest is tended
> In ways that it cannot intend
> Is borne, preserved, and comprehended
> By what it cannot comprehend.[8]

Hopefully we don't have to have a bullet in the brain like Harrison Ford in *Regarding Henry* before we learn the value of slowing down. God's gift of rest and re-creation is calling us today, holding out its hand, inviting us to enter into its easy and grace-filled dance. And as we learn to move with the beauty of its restful rhythm, we will find ourselves feeling more alive, looking more closely at the people right around us, digging more deeply into the natural resources of our special circumstances. We will learn to mine the gentle, restful treasures of our very own lives, right where we are. As we open our hearts to embrace God's Sabbath opportunities, we will be discovering this delightful and free ing reality—that earth's apron is covered with little pockets of heaven's rest for those who will stop to find them.

9

A Childlike Heart

When we are truly in this interior simplicity our whole appearance is franker, more natural. This true simplicity . . . makes us conscious of a certain openness, gentleness, innocence, gaiety, and serenity, which is charming when we see it near to and continually, with pure eyes.

—François Fènelon

I've wasted a lot of time in my life wishing I could be like someone else.

In seventh grade, for instance, I wanted to be like Melinda Felker. She had dark, almost almond-shaped eyes, and I thought she was mysterious. Don't ask me why I thought I had to be mysterious in the seventh grade. I just liked the way it looked on Melinda.

In high school, I wanted to be short and shapely like my best friend, Linda Lee Ricketts, instead of tall and angular like my dad. Linda Lee had that Sandra Dee look that was so very much in vogue during the late 1950s and early 1960s. She was cute and cuddly. I was all knees and elbows.

If I could have taken all the qualities I admired in others and added them to my own package of qualities, like oregano added to a pan of pasta sauce, I would have done it. I wanted Judy's personality and Charlotte's sense of style and Kathleen's energy and Gisti's complexion. I wanted to take the best parts of all my friends and tack them on to me like a Victorian porch on a ranch-style house or a ruffly apron on a jogging suit.

Why did it take me so long to want to be me?

A Unique Design

Many of us, instead of maturing into our own best selves, have tried to add on "improvements" that were never meant to be part of our basic model. We've spent a lot of time and energy trying to remake the original concept into what the world values. But nothing could be more exhausting than spending every day trying to be what we're not. It's a waste of time, and it's also something of a slap in the face of the One who designed us!

God made each of us a true original. Psalm 139 reminds us that he knitted each of us together inside of our mother's body. Every stitch was carefully considered and executed. He didn't goof up and make you by mistake. You're the one he wanted, the one he designed, the one he brought into being . . . on purpose! So am I.

There is nothing more freeing than deciding to reconnect with and embrace the self that God designed us to be. On my journey to a place called Simplicity, I have been learning to value God's basic design, the original me I was meant to be.

All of us started out pretty simple. In fact, what could be simpler than the package we arrived in? Is there anything complex about a baby's approach to life? He cries when he's hungry, sleeps when he's sleepy, and lets you know in no uncertain terms when he's wet and uncomfortable. He hasn't discovered yet how to have an identity crisis. He is very simply himself.

A Childlike Heart

Jesus loved what he saw when he looked into the faces of children. He even listed the quality of childlikeness as a prerequisite for kingdom membership: "Let the little children come to me, and do not hinder them, for the kingdom of God belongs to such as these. I tell you the truth, anyone who will not receive the kingdom of God like a little child will never enter it" (Mark 10:14,15).

A Journey of Rediscovery

Who were you as a little child? Have you thought about that lately? What kind of a baby did you start out as? Find an old photograph of yourself as an infant or a toddler and look into that trusting little face. Or take the time to ask some questions and explore some memories. You may be surprised at what you will discover.

Several years ago my sister Ann and I found ourselves on just such a nostalgic pilgrimage, "searching for our childhood." It all began at the fiftieth anniversary party my siblings and I hosted for Mom and Dad (an intimate little gathering for just seven hundred of their closest friends!). The party was crowded with old teachers and friends and neighbors from the past, and Ann and I found ourselves madly reminiscing all day long as we renewed friendships and smiled into old, familiar faces. That was when we decided to spend the whole next day "going back in time" and looking for those two little blonde-haired girls we used to be.

What a crazy experience! We started at our old elementary school, F.M. Hamilton. There was the entrance to the auditorium where Miss Cox, the music teacher, used to lead the student body in that old favorite, "Stodala-Pumpa." Upstairs was the library where our favorite librarian, Miss Carstens, transported us to different worlds through the stories she read. There was the basement window that Ann and Flossie Fava jumped out of

A Childlike Heart

with Mr. Pete, the school janitor, in hot pursuit. There was the Brownie Hut where Linda Bernard and I invariably got kicked out of the scout meetings for talking and giggling when we should have been working on our badges.

Just a block away from school we located a truly historic childhood landmark, the little building that once housed Rachou's Grocery. Rachou's was where kids would send "Skinny Bones" Connelly off campus during recess with their money to purchase wax lips and teeth. You could only get them in the spring. (I don't think anyone makes wax lips and teeth anymore, and if they don't, it's a real shame. They were one of the highlights of our childhood!)

But the best part of our nostalgic journey was our trip to the old neighborhood. There was our old house—with a slight face-lift and a bold new paint job, but still our old house.

"Look!" Ann screamed, pointing at the cracks in the front sidewalk. "Remember these?" We were amazed at how familiar those spidery little cracks seemed after all these years! We had both learned to walk on that sidewalk, and we had traveled its familiar surfaces, coming and going, for all of our elementary school years.

The next thing we knew, we were knocking on the familiar front door of 135 Clark Court, hoping the current owners would have pity on us and invite us in. No answer. We were disappointed, but not daunted. By standing on our tiptoes and smashing our noses against the screen windows, we could catch just a glimpse of the living room through the inside drapes.

That was when the big blue van driven by the new homeowner pulled into the driveway.

She was a little suspicious at first. But we apologized profusely and explained who we were and hung around looking so hopeful that she ended up asking us

A Childlike Heart

in. Ann grabbed my hand and we stepped through the front door. Neither of us said a word for a hushed moment. We were looking around as wide-eyed as Hansel and Gretel in the gingerbread house.

Then it began: "Remember when we dressed the twins up like Captain Hook and Wendy? Remember when Mama made a Superman cape for the pet rooster? Remember the treehouse in the oak tree... and Jeannie Dulaney's ringlets... and the Arbolada Gang?"

We went from room to room, whispering and giggling and feeling like kids, letting each room recall another memory and each memory another story. Most of the house had been remodeled, but a few things had not been changed. The molding around the floors and ceiling and fireplace was the way we remembered it. The knotty pine paneling in the den had been painted over, but the knots were still there! The tile in the bathrooms was exactly the same.

Then something amazing hit me like a ton of bricks, right in the middle of all the emotion and all the memories. I realized that even under all this remodeling, it really was still the same house! These were the same floors we had walked around on, the same windows we had looked out of growing up.

But more than that. It also hit me that under all of our grown-up clothes and our makeup and our education and experiences, Ann and I were still the same little girls—the same little tow-headed, mischievous kids who had grown up here all those years ago.

I was suddenly filled with a warmth and a love not only for my little sister, but (strangely) for myself as a child. I was deeply touched by the innocence and hope and vulnerability we had possessed as children, and I recognized its value. I couldn't quite articulate what I was feeling at the time, but I think I know now what it was.

A Childlike Heart

Still inside of Ann and me and each of us is the tender, awkward, innocent child we left back in our childhood. And that child, whoever he or she was, is very precious indeed to God the Father. There are childlike qualities that we've somehow lost by living in this fallen' world—qualities he would like to help us reclaim. Ir fact, there is something about childhood that car actually be the key to our discovery of a simpler self.

Lessons in Simplicity

Why did Jesus use childlikeness as a prerequisite to kingdom membership? What did he really mean when he invited us to come to him as children? Is it really possible for those of us who live in a grown-up world to he childlike again? I believe these questions are road signs that can lead us to some valuable lessons in simplicity as we look at some of the qualities that Jesus treasured in children.

Children Grow

One reason it is so exciting to be around little children is that they are so obviously works in progress. They are in the process of becoming, and they grow a little more each day. When we are with our nephew, Kappel, and his little sister, Lilly, I can almost feel that process taking place in their lives right in front of our eyes! They are so bright and funny and full of energy, it is as though I can hear them saying, "Stick around and stay tuned! You don't want to miss this! No telling what we'll be into by this afternoon!"

When children are growing as God intended, it's a dynamic thing. Their bodies are growing taller and stronger. Their minds are expanding to take in and understand more. Their spirits are opening like flowers in the sunshine. When we have simple, childlike hearts, we're like that, too. We continue to grow, to learn, to stretch, to mature. We don't stagnate. We don't reach the "know it all" state. We stay excited about being alive.

My mom and dad are inspirations to me because they are still very much in a growth pattern. Daddy turned eighty years old last weekend, but I don't think for a minute that he sees himself as "old." He's self-employed and still working; he's involved in politics; he has worlds of friends; he loves to play the piano and organ; he exercises every day. When Mom was in her sixties, she decided to go back to school and get her Ph.D. in psychology. Now, at age seventy-eight, she is a counselor who sees clients every day! She loves pretty clothes, is an avid reader, and is a close personal friend to each of her children, grandchildren, and great-grandchildren. It's exciting to be with Mom and Dad because they haven't let being grown up get in the way of their growing!

Scripture tells us that growth is part of God's purpose for us. He desires for us to be conformed to the likeness of his Son (Romans 8:29), by continually growing into his image (2 Corinthians 3:18). This means that even as we leave "childish things" behind and grow toward maturity, we can continue to be child*like*—still in the process of becoming the people God created us to be.

Children Understand Joy

One of the reasons we adults love to take children to amusement parks is that children give us permission to enter into the joy of the moment. Children don't waste an opportunity for joy. They take full advantage of the attractions, and they help us to do the same.

But it certainly doesn't take a big, shiny theme park to delight a little child. Something small can bring enormous pleasure to a child's heart. Have you ever noticed a baby on Christmas morning, for instance? While the adults are exclaiming over the gifts, baby's over in the corner delighting in the cast-off wrapping paper!

A Childlike Heart

I used to be a little baffled by Nehemiah 8:10: "For the joy of the Lord is your strength." To me, that verse never made much sense, because joy didn't seem to be all that strong a quality. I thought it would have made more sense if it had said, "The *strength* of the Lord is your *joy*."

But the longer I live, the more I realize that the ability to find joy in life really is a tremendous strength. The people who can laugh are the strong ones. The people who can throw their heads back and delight in the joy of the moment are going to live a lot longer than the ones of us who are stressed and pushed and taking ourselves terribly seriously.

On a recent canoe trip to North Carolina with friends, Spike was strengthened and buoyed by the childlike joy of a wonderful moment. Here is how he recorded it in his journal:

> Somewhere near the beginning of my river run, while I was still fine-tuning my paddling technique and becoming comfortable with the river and its forces, I heard behind me a joyous tumult of laughter from an oncoming raft. . . . I turned just in time to see a large raft filled to overflowing with madly paddling youngsters, all of them in full-throated laughter.
>
> It was a raft full of Down Syndrome kids out for a day on the river. Truly uninhibited joy that is rarely seen except in tiny children was erupting in their voices and on their faces. They were feeding upon the moment with such abandon that all else was swept away. Their whole focus, their whole life was right here. Right now. And the power of it was unconquerable, sweeping up everything within the sound of their voices into an all-encompassing joy.

As they flashed past me I caught the eyes of the ones who could see me.... And reflected back at me was such clear and complete love and acceptance of all that they were, this moment, this second, this day. ... "We are here, and you are too, and it is all so very wonderful and grand and not to be contained," their eyes seemed to say as they swept past me, laughing and shouting and splashing their paddles and bouncing down the current and around the bend.

"Thank you!" I shouted and raised my paddle high in salute to their joy and grace. And wisdom.[1]

Obviously, Spike learned a beautiful lesson from those handicapped children in the raft. Their contagious joy freed him to celebrate his own day with a measure of abandon he might not otherwise have been able to manage.

Children really are good at open-hearted, spontaneous joy. They know it intuitively. That's why they use it lavishly in the present moment. They don't put it in a saving's account for a rainy day. They don't put it on hold or put a lid on it. They spend it with abandon. They practice it at every small occasion. That's why they are such pros at getting it right! They automatically take the advice that was once rushed to writer Tim Hansel in a telegram: "Until further notice, celebrate everything!"[2]

Children Are Honest and Transparent

When I say that children are honest, I don't mean for a minute that they won't tell an occasional lie. Most of them will do that once in a while, some with great imagination and skill. What I *do* mean is that children wear their hearts on their sleeves. They have not yet learned to

A Childlike Heart

wear masks and disguises. They have not perfected the art of putting up a good front or manipulating the data to slant the story. They are who they are, and who they are comes out clearly in their speech and their actions.

Quite a few years ago now, my friends Mallie and Danny took their children to meet Danny's elderly Aunt Ella Mae, who had lost both her arms long years before in a childhood accident. Before the visit, Mallie and Danny carefully explained the situation and cautioned the children to spare Aunt Ella Mae's feelings by not mentioning her deformity.

"Now, remember what I said," Mallie drilled them one more time as they approached their destination. "Don't mention the fact that she has no arms. Just don't say anything about it."

Both Mallie and Danny were a little apprehensive as they introduced the children to their elderly relative for the first time, but the children were very polite. They said their quiet hellos and then found some toys in the den to play with while the grown-ups talked in the living room. For a while, it actually seemed that a potentially embarrassing moment had been avoided. Both parents began to breathe easier.

And then suddenly Mallie looked up in horror to see her children at the living room door. They had pulled their arms out of the sleeves of their little T-shirts. Slowly and rhythmically, they walked single file into the living room, their empty sleeves flapping at their sides like silent reproaches!

Mallie still cringes when she remembers that moment. She has realized since that day, however, that she should never have expected her children to repress their natural curiosity about Aunt Ella Mae. Children are far too honest to be coy or diplomatic—or even polite, if being polite calls for deception. When we teach them to mask their honesty, we are teaching them to lie. Mallie now realizes she would have been much better off if she had allowed the children to talk to Aunt Ella Mae honestly about their questions and feelings.

Believe it or not, God values childlike openness far more than he values false social proprieties. He doesn't acknowledge "little white lies"; to him, all of them are black. In Matthew 5:37, Jesus counsels all who would live as children of the kingdom to speak plainly and forthrightly, letting "your 'Yes' be 'Yes,' and your 'No,' 'No.'"

In a world that has carefully schooled us to cloak our language in different nuances for different occasions (business, social, spiritual, romantic), we may find the simplicity of plain talk a bit uncomfortable at first. But as we get better at it, we will most likely discover that it brings with it new levels of inner peace and simplicity. When our language is washed with honesty, it will never be falsely flattering. And when our honesty is motivated by love, the truth we speak will build people up and not tear them down. With practice, we may find a whole new freedom in reclaiming the childlike virtue of saying what we mean and meaning what we say!

Children Have a Natural Sense of Awe and Wonder

So many of us in our culture have become jaded about life. The overload of information and stimulation we're exposed to daily has stripped us of the ability to react with amazement even about amazing things. Sometimes I look at children and envy the eyes that see everything as new.

Some years ago, on one of the historic nights that Haley's Comet was to be visible in the night sky over Mobile, our friends Bradley and Rebecca woke their little son Patrick and whisked him out into the darkness to view the heavenly spectacle. Patrick's reaction? He was unabashedly awed.

"Oh, Mommy," he whispered, "I'm afraid." Rebecca could tell by his countenance that he was not actually fearful, but was instead trying to express his amazement. His parents' hushed and reverent tones as they explained this rare phenomenon had tipped him off to the fact that he was about to see something wondrous and special, and the closest word he had for being awe-struck was "afraid."

I really believe this is what the Bible is talking about when it says that "the fear of the Lord is the beginning of wisdom" (Psalm 111:10). A very loose modern trans-lation of that verse might be, "If you're smart, you'll realize what an awesome God you serve!"

Spike tends to be very childlike in the wonder and awe department—that's one of the things I love about him. Just a minute ago he knocked on my office door and came in bearing a perfect, almost neon-colored "Cha-risma" rose from a bush that was my anniversary pres-ent a few years before. The amazed expression on his face was childlike indeed He loves for me to delight with him in treasures of his day. And I have no doubt that Spike's perspective of wonder delights the Father, too. In an age of disenchantment and sophistication, Spike's childlike view of the world around him is a rare and precious commodity!

Children Freely Trust That Their Needs Will Be Met

I heard Christian singer, Steven Curtis Chapman, tell this anecdote about his little girl recently, and it spoke volumes to me about trust: One night while Steven and Mary Beth were entertaining company in the living room, they heard a thumping sound, and looked up to see their little girl bumping down the stairs on her bot-tom with her panties around her ankles, a wad of toilet paper clutched tightly in her little fist. While her slightly shocked parents and their guests looked on, she wad-dled up to Steven, handed him the toilet paper, and said, "Here, Daddy, help me."

Steven admits that there was a brief moment of awkwardness—for everyone but his little girl. She was perfectly confident throughout the whole incident. And the more he thought about it, the more it struck him that she was the one who had the right attitude. She had done exactly what he would have wanted her to do. She knew where she could go for the help she needed, and she wasn't too shy to ask!

Do we feel this comfortable about going to our heavenly parent for help? We are his kids. But are we holding back, afraid to trust his provision? Are we still trying to meet our own needs even though he has invited us to burst through his doors and into his presence at any time of the night or day with whatever problem we have? (Hebrews 4:16 says that we can "approach the throne of grace with confidence, so that we may receive mercy and find grace to help us in our time of need.")

Little children know all too well that they need their parents. They cannot walk into a bank and cash a check. They can't drive a car or earn a living. They are totally dependent on their parents' care. Spiritual simplicity is realizing we all really are this dependent on God, whatever our age or station in life. If we tell ourselves we don't really need him, we're not only being arrogant, but also self-deceptive—like rebellious teenagers who think they're totally independent but still show up at home for three meals a day.

There is no pride or self-sufficiency in a true child of the kingdom; he relies wholly on the faithfulness and the mercies of God. I believe it is this kind of childlike humility that the first beatitude is talking about when it says, "Blessed are the poor in spirit" (Matthew 5:3). It is to the poor in spirit, who come readily to their heavenly Dad with their needs, that he promises total rights to "the kingdom of heaven."

Like Spike on the river, Harvard theology professor and author Henri Nouwen learned volumes about childlike simplicity from the mentally handicapped. Longing for a simpler, more communal life than his academic existence offered, Nouwen surprised his associates by leaving Harvard in 1985 to live among a small community of mentally handicapped adults in Trosley, France.

After only a short time in Trosley, Nouwen was learning more about faith from the gentle lives of these childlike people than he felt he had been able to communicate to his own students during all of his years at Harvard. In this passage from his book, *The Road to Daybreak*, Nouwen describes what he learned from Danny, one of the men in the community.

> Danny said, "I love you, Jesus. I do not reject you even when i get nervous once in a while . . . even when I get confused. I love you with my arms, my legs, my head, my heart; I love you and I do not reject you, Jesus. I know that you love me, that you love me so much. I love you, too, Jesus." As he prayed, I looked at his beautiful, gentle face and saw without any veil or cover his agony as well as his love. . . . I suddenly felt a deep desire to invite all my students from Harvard to sit with me there in that circle. . . . I wanted so much for all of them to sit and let Danny tell them about Jesus.[3]

We, too, could learn much from Danny. Not that we have to be mentally challenged to have that kind of simple faith, any more than we have to revert to childhood to recover a childlike simplicity. But sometimes we can become so bogged down in theological mazes that we forget where the Center is. And it doesn't have to be that way. Danny reminds us that we can bypass all the mental obstacle courses we sometimes run and approach Jesus from the heart, with simplicity and openness.

Children Know Who They Are
and Whose They Are

A little child who is loved is comfortable in her skin. She never worries if her slip is showing or if she's saying the right thing at the right time. She knows that Mama and Daddy love her and that they're close by. That is why she is able to be herself with confidence . . . her real self.

Sadly, none of us (even from the best of families) receives the measure of pure, unconditional love required for maintaining this level of childlike self-confidence. By the time most of us hit school age, we are already suspecting that we're "not okay." We're already struggling to fit in, wishing we could change who we are so that we can be more like someone we admire. We're already learning to work for the approval of others.

The only way that any of us will ever be able to regain that childlike sense of who we are and what we were designed to be is by opening our hearts to the unconditional love that is able to make us real again. Only as we allow the love of Christ to penetrate our wounds will we be able to love again as children love. Only as we open ourselves to the love of Christ and his people can we begin our journey toward being real.

Getting back to real is not an overnight journey. Letting the Lord love the sophistication of the world's message out of us is a lifetime proposition. As Margery Williams put it in *The Velveteen Rabbit*, "It takes a long time. . . . Generally by the time you are Real, most of your hair has been loved off, and your eyes drop out and you get loose in the joints and very shabby. But these things don't matter at all, because once you are Real you can't be ugly . . . [and] you can't become unreal again. It lasts for always."[4]

My own deep yearning for a "real" childlike heart inspired me to write this song which closes with a one-line prayer for us all:

Where is that girl that you used to be,
The one with the bruises and scrapes on her
   knee,
The one who wore feelings and faith on her
   sleeve—
Where is that precious child?

Where is that boy who loved a surprise,
Who had pockets of wishes and dreams in
   his eyes,
Who loved to make pictures of clouds in the
   skies—
Where is that precious child?

How did all the work and worry
Bury the hope and trust?
Listen to Jesus; He's calling us back,
Back to the child in us.

Where is that child that yesterday knew?
Where are those feelings so simple and true?
Jesus is beckoning me and you
Back to that precious child.
Lord, take me back to that precious child.[5]

All of us are invited into a faith relationship with Jesus Christ that can redeem our sin-distorted selves and restore us to the new-birth experience of being children in his kingdom. Realizing that he loves us totally, right down to the essence of who we are, heals us and frees us to risk being simpler selves. Allowing him to show us that the bottom layer of who we are in him has more beauty about it than the top layer of our favorite masquerade empowers us to drop our disguises and enter into the simple beauty of his life.

10
A Simple Faith

*B*ut slowly I came to see that God desired to be not on the outskirts, but at the heart of my experience. Gardening was no longer an experience outside of my relationship with God—I discovered God in the gardening. Swimming was no longer just good exercise—it became an opportunity for communion with God. God in Christ had become the center.

—Richard J. Foster

To me, one of the spookiest moments in all science fiction filmdom occurs in a movie entitled *The Stepford Wives.* The movie is about a men's-only club in the classy suburb of Stepford whose members are dedicated to killing off all the wives in the community and replacing each woman with a cosmetically perfect, more docile and domestic facsimile of herself.

Toward the end of the movie, there is a bizarre scene in which the audience first realizes that one of the heroines (played by Paula Prentiss) has been replaced by a robot double. In this scene, the Prentiss robot sustains an injury to her flawless facade that reveals not flesh and blood beneath, but a now-damaged inner mechanism. The wounded robot wife, her circuitry gone haywire, goes bustling back and forth about her perfect kitchen—bumping into counters, pulling packages off of shelves, mechanically dumping out their contents, and chirping cheerful but inappropriate little "wifey" remarks to no one in particular.

A lot of moviegoers may have found that scene ridiculous. But I got a real case of the creeps watching it, probably because it carried an element of *déjà vous* for me. It reminded me of myself on days when I've felt as if my wiring had finally popped and left me in a state of active chaos—bustling back and forth through a lot of meaningless activities, meeting myself coming and going, not accomplishing a thing or making any real connection with anyone.

On crazy days like that, I'd almost rather *be* a robot. If we were robots, it would all be so simple. We could just go in for a tune-up and get a few wires tweaked, and everything would be swell.

But we are not robots. We are complex people living in a complex world. The apple has been eaten, the Garden has shut down, and at any given time the chaos is closing in on all sides!

So, realistically speaking, where do we actually start this journey to a place called Simplicity? We've agreed that the simplifying choice is ours, and perhaps now we're even ready to begin making it. We've talked about simplicity in terms of our time and our leisure and our homes. We've considered our need for simplicity in managing our money and our work. We've talked about adopting a simpler, more childlike approach to life, and perhaps we've even caught a glimpse of something more sane and more serene. But where do we go from here? How can we set our inner mechanisms aright so that we can stop all this pointless bumping and bustling and begin to live in the simplicity we are beginning to believe is possible?

Simplicity Is an Inside Job

Because I am an action person, my first inclination would be to rush to the starting line and begin cleaning out closets and cutting up credit cards. But I know by now that outward attempts to effect change rarely transform the inner person. The only shot any of us have at real change is to go at it from the other direction: from the inside out.

In his letter to the Colossians, Paul reminds us that we who follow Christ have died to the outward attempts, to the world's little stopgap list of do's and don'ts: "'Do not handle! Do not taste! Do not touch!' These are all destined to perish with use," he says, "because they are based on human commands and teachings. Such regulations indeed have an appearance of wisdom . . . but they lack any value in restraining sensual indulgence" (2:21-23).

Exercising our willpower on our outward circumstances and behavior will never bring the level of genuine simplicity that our spirits crave. "In the cracks and crevices of our lives our deep inner condition will eventually be revealed."[1] The impeccable closets we have so rigorously organized will spring leaks of disorder. The balanced budget will lose its balance. And, to paraphrase Robert Burns, the simplest plans of mice and men will go chaotic.

Simplicity cannot be worked up or attained or willed or worried into being. External measures prove worse than no good at all. This is why the first step on the road to Simplicity is not to move into a frenzy of activity, but rather to *slow down*.

A Simple Faith

Come into the Quiet

Simplicity begins with finding some times to be alone with the Lord, times for being still and allowing him to quiet our inner beings. "In quietness and in confidence shall be your strength," the prophet Isaiah reminds us (30:15 KJV). For only in the quiet will we find the spiritual resources to act on Paul's invitation: "Do not conform any longer to the pattern of this world, but be transformed by the renewing of your mind" (Romans 12:2).

In the quiet, our restless minds can begin to be renewed. Our compulsive selves—the selves that are constantly pushing for affirmation and attention, the selves that begin every sentence with the pronoun *I*, the selves that have lost their aptitude for contentment—can begin to be tamed.

And in the quiet, the Spirit of God can begin to wash away what is false and superfluous in us. He can remove the noisy, busy layers of our striving so that we can begin to reflect the peace of the One who is perfect Peace. For as Gerhardt Tersteegen has said, "God is a tranquil Being, and abides in a tranquil eternity. So must thy spirit become a tranquil and clear little pool, wherein the serene light of God can be mirrored."[2]

Simplicity Is a Person

In the silence, once the restlessness of our inner selves has been stilled, we can see with clear eyes and a quiet spirit that simple reality we've been rushing right past every day. It is this: Simplicity is not a state of mind. It is not a method of housekeeping or bookkeeping or appointment keeping. It is not a philosophy or a theology or an ancient art form or a new ecological movement. Simplicity is a person, and his name is Jesus.

Jesus is the One of whom the twelfth-century monk, Bernard of Clairvaux, spoke when he said, "So long,

A Simple Faith

then, as I am not united to [Him], I am divided within myself and at perpetual strife within myself."[3] Jesus was the key to inner harmony in the twelfth-century, and he still is today.

Jesus is the one who said of himself, "I am the way and the truth and the life" (John 14:6). He is the way to a place called Simplicity; he is the strong, grace-filled foundational truth that we are seeking in our quest for a simpler life; and he is the life itself, the life of simplicity that we so desperately desire.

Jesus said that if we will only seek him first, everything will be so much simpler—that everything we need will be added to us (see Matthew 6:33). But by "seek... first" he did not mean simply putting him at the top of a crowded "to do" list, spending a few perfunctory minutes a day reading a few verses or mumbling a few petitions and then scratching him off the list in order to get on with the rushed and compulsive rest of our lives. Jesus did not come to be just one more item on our agenda —"not even the most important item. He did not come... to be the most crucial piece of our fragmented life; He came to absorb *all* of life—our family, job, talents, dreams, ministry—into Himself and impress on it His mark."[4]

To tack Christ onto an already crammed agenda is to further complicate our lives, whereas to allow his love to absorb us totally is to simplify our lives. As we seek him first in our quiet moments, we are giving him the opportunity to absorb the restless rhythms of who we are into the amazing peace of who he is.

He is the God who has decreed that we set aside special times to work and to worship, special times to rest and rejoice and be restored, and he longs for us to find our quiet center of gravity in him. Where our lives have become unbalanced, he longs to bring his perfect balance. Where our lives have become disordered, he longs to supply his order. Where our schedules and our relationships and values have become tangled, he longs to comb through them with his grace and set them aright.

An Ever-Deepening Relationship

As we grow willing to come into the quiet and spend time with the Lord, we will find ourselves being drawn into an ever-deepening relationship with him. We will be drawn from the outward reality of his transcendence . . . to an awareness of his presence all around us . . . and finally to an inward revelation of him as our indwelling and abiding life.

The Transcendent One: God Above Us

Jesus is the transcendent One who is over us and over all creation. Unlike the small "self-gods" of this naval-gazing culture, who are supposed to lie within our unredeemed humanity waiting to serve us like personal genies, Jesus is first of all the God above us. He is a fully functioning part of the Creator God who was here from the foundations of the world (see John 1). He is the great, exalted One to whom God has given all power and authority and under whose feet God has put all things (see 1 Corinthians 15:24,27). He is the One who bears the name of the new Jerusalem, who sits at the right hand of God (see Revelation 3:12,21).

Last summer at a Christian music conference in the mountains of Colorado, I really got in touch with Jesus as the transcendent Christ who is over all. It all began when Curt, Andy, and Jenni decided to take me along on an adventure—an expedition to "experience the mountains" after dark. Following someone's recommendation, we drove up a gravel road that seemed to go straight up the side of a mountain.

As we ascended, the light of day seemed gradually to evaporate, leaving us in pitch darkness. I had the feeling that we had been transported to some alien planet. A luminescent silver semicircle of a moon was rising in a black velvet sky, and we could feel the huge, jutting forms of mountains looming all around us.

It is difficult to describe the intense mixture of terror and wonder I felt. Suddenly I was very aware that there was no guard rail to keep us on track! Our headlights cast a small pool of light just ahead, but we couldn't tell which way the road would turn next.

I have never been more tuned in to the reality of my smallness and the Lord's greatness than I was that night. As we drove, it occurred to me how lost and helpless we would feel in a universe without our loving Savior who is over all. How good it is to know that he can always see the road ahead of us, even when we can't. How good to know that we are held in his mighty and compassionate hands!

As we reached the top of the mountain, as we looked up at the stars and out at the shadows of the mountains all around us, we were overwhelmed by the majestic beauty. Very softly we began to sing, "Oh, Lord, you're beautiful!"

Understanding our smallness in relation to his greatness can be an important key in our relationship with Jesus, for it puts things in proper perspective. As Oswald Chambers has said, "I cannot enter His Kingdom as a good man or woman, I can only enter it as a complete pauper."[5] In addition, acknowledging Jesus as the God above us often brings forth a response of praise, as it did in us that night. This in turn draws him into our lives in a strong and present way, for he inhabits the praises of his people (Psalm 22:3 KJV).

Emmanuel: God with Us and Among Us

Although Jesus is the transcendent One, with the Father from the beginning, he has not been content to remain above and beyond us. For he is also Emmanuel, the God who drew near. The miracle of Bethlehem is that the Creator entered his own creation and lived among his creatures as one of them. One of us! He forever elevated the status of human beings by being clothed in humanity for our sakes. He became connected to us as a member of the human family. He became a Son and a Brother and a Neighbor and a Friend.

Only last week I had a new insight into Christ's being one of us. It began with a collect call from our twenty-four-year-old son, Curt. (My mom says you know kids are finally, really grown when they stop calling collect, but she cautioned me not to hold my breath!) Curt and I can really run up the phone bill, because we love to get into long conversations about what the Lord has been teaching us lately.

"What's going on with you this week?" I asked.

"It's really great," he answered. "I'm getting closer to Jesus—the Jesus who was a man. I think I'm getting a clearer sense of who he was than I've ever had before."

"How?" I asked.

"Well, I've been seeing him like a big brother. It's something I've never thought of before. I've never had a big brother, and I always envied guys who did. I never had an older guy I could really trust and turn to. And all week long, I've been thinking of him like that. Realizing that he's there for me like that. As a brother."

After we hung up, I thought a lot about what Curt had said. I even tried to think of Jesus as my big brother, but I couldn't get it to work for me. And then I realized why. Jesus was thirty-three when he died. I'm a good decade and a half older than that.

That's when it hit me. Mary was probably just about my age when Jesus was crucified. I got a shiver down my spine thinking how awful it must have been for her. I thought of my own two sons and how much I love them and how devastating it would be to see them suffer and die. In my quiet time the next day, I reread the crucifixion passages and sat in silence reflecting on Jesus as a man, a human being—someone's son, someone's brother, someone's friend.

How blessed we are to have a God who came and lived right here among us! And how amazing to realize that he has risen and is alive and is among us still! He's even told us that whenever two or three gather in his name, he is here. Right where we are.

This is the song I wrote after that quiet time of reflecting on Jesus' humanity, his willingness to share in our experience, his painful death, his resurrection, and his present-moment nearness to those who worship him:

> Two or three or more have gathered
> As a family, drawing near,
> Bringing every expectation,
> Knowing that you meet us here.
>
> Right where we are, right where we are,
> The glory of your love is shining
> Brighter than the brightest star.
> Right where we are, right where we are,
> The mercy of your love is reaching
> Into every waiting heart...
> Right where we are.
>
> For we know your Word is with us
> In our hearts and in our mouths,
> And your Holy Spirit fills us
> As we praise you here and now.[6]

The Glorious Mystery: God Within Us

But Jesus desires to be even closer to us than a brother or a friend. He is not only the God who is above us and the God who has come among us; he is also the

God who desires to dwell within us. This is the fact that the Apostle Paul described in Colossians 1:27 as "the glorious . . . mystery, which is Christ in you, the hope of glory." It is the wonder he describes in Galatians 2:20 when he says, "I have been crucified with Christ and I no longer live, but Christ lives in me."

This is the mystery we were made to contain: the very life of Jesus. He means to live out the reality of who he is right here within the reality of who we are. He means to be our lives—the breath in our lungs, the thoughts in our heads, the energy and creativity in our jobs, the love in our hearts. He means to take on the stress and unravel the inner complications so that we can move through our lives just as he did, in gentleness and simplicity and harmony.

We were never intended to be more than containers: temples to contain his glory (1 Corinthians 3:16,17), branches to contain the sap of his life (John 15:1-8), vessels to contain the new wine of his Spirit (Romans 9:20,21). We are the glove; he is the hand. We are the cup; he is the coffee. We are the lamp; he is the light.

This is what we were made for. This is the intended purpose of the human person and personality: not to be gods, but to contain God. This is the kind of unity that was present in the Garden but that is sadly missing in this world. It is the sheer simplicity of God's design that was shattered by humanity's sin. And it is the reason that Jesus came and cared and was tortured and killed and laid in a tomb and raised to life again . . . so that he could give us another shot at being what we were intended to be.

Do you know why it's so hard for us to be simple here on planet Earth? It's because we are trying to do a job we were never meant to do. Every morning that we wake up and take the reins of our own lives into our own hands and start making all the decisions and calling all the shots, we are trying to do God's job. And every time we do, it is pretty much a foregone conclusion that sooner or later we will end up bruised and confused.

Experiencing His Life

Have you ever experienced what it's like to let Jesus take over in you for an hour or a day or a week? Have you ever felt the tremendous release that comes from realizing that the Lord is actually carrying you through a time of confusion or stress or trial? You knew you couldn't do it, so you called on him, and suddenly he was there doing what he promised he would do!

I recently had an experience like that. I had just spent the better part of two months completing a choir musical that I had been commissioned to do—ten songs and a dramatic script. I thought, based on what I had been told, that my musical was right in the ball park with what the publisher needed. But one person in a key decision-making position at the publishing company had been out of town when all of our discussion about the musical's direction was taking place. When he returned and read my script, he telephoned me and kindly but firmly let me know that what I had done was not going to fit the slot they needed to fill. I would have to go back to the drawing board, he said. And since we had gotten a late start anyway, he was afraid that I only had about ten days to come up with a whole new musical.

I had been under a lot of stress anyway, juggling several different deadlines for other projects, and I had been so relieved to have the musical completed. Now this! I could feel a whole army of stressful emotions waiting to pounce on me. Anger, self-pity, panic, despair. Then, just as I was about to give in to this deluge of feelings, I heard the Lord whisper to me, "Let me take this for you, Claire. I will, if you'll let me."

I had just been reading the little book about the life of Brother Lawrence, *The Practice of the Presence of God*, and it was lying open on my desk right next to the telephone. So instead of beginning to rage or sob or tear my hair or kick the dog (all of which felt like appropriate responses to my publisher's phone call) I picked up that little book and read these words: "When he had business to do, he did not think of it beforehand; but when it was time to do it God showed him, as in a mirror, how it should be done. For some time he had followed this plan of not anticipating difficulties."[7]

As I closed the book and sank into the big, blue easy chair in my office, I was filled with the awareness that I didn't have to give in to my emotions. I could turn them over. It was my option.

"Lord," I prayed, "I don't feel that I have any more energy or ideas left in me to write another musical. But I know that you have all the energy and ideas I could ever need. If you want me to write another musical, I will. If this is what you want, then I'm asking you to do it in me. I'm going to give you this whole flood of emotion that's trying to engulf me now. Lord, come live this situation out in me. Be my serenity. I know you want to, and I believe you can." Then I sat there for a long time just feeling these waves of peace come over me.

Spike knew I had been on the phone with my publisher and was waiting to hear how they liked the musical. As I walked into the house, he took one look at my tranquil, smiling face and said, "They loved it!"

"No," I said. "They hated it. I have to do it over. But it's okay. I'm going to get some sleep tonight and take another look at it tomorrow."

That really blew him away. Ordinarily, I would have been out of control, to say the least. But there I was, walking around in my right mind! I think he was further amazed to watch me walk through the rest of the ordeal with the amount of peace that I had. Of course, that's because I wasn't the one walking through it. It really was Jesus in me.

I did finish the second version of the musical, and that in itself was a pretty big miracle. But to me, the bigger miracle by far was the experience of Christ giving me his serenity and his emotional strength. For ten days I was carried. He was with me in the writing and the resting, nearer than my heartbeat. He kept me together and at peace in a situation that would ordinarily have caused me to give up or give in.

The Bottom Holds

Whenever I have experienced his indwelling presence the way I did when I was writing the musical, I find myself wondering why I would ever choose to live any other way. Why would I ever return to living in my own strength?

Sadly, though, it has only been in real times of trouble or stress or grief that I have been pressed enough really to "let go and let God." It has only been when I knew my back was against the wall and I simply couldn't make it on my own that I have released my grip and felt him catch me. But every time I've done that, he has been right there.

It is like the story our friend John Barr used to tell about the dean of his seminary, whose precious son commited suicide. Dean Trotter was scheduled to preach only a few weeks after the funeral, but most of the seminarians speculated he would choose not to preach so soon—not while his grief was still so fresh. On the scheduled Sunday, however, Dean Trotter was in chapel. After the sermon hymn, he rose slowly and walked with determination to the pulpit. Very quietly, he looked out over the faces of the professors and students who had been praying for his family throughout his ordeal.

"I come to report to you," he said softly, "that I have been to the bottom. And it holds."

When we are at the bottom and we seem to have no other choice, we do lean into God's power. That is when we are willing to be filled and indwelt. We know we can't live our own lives, and so we are willing to give Christ a shot at doing it in us. But all too often, when the crisis is past, we thank him politely, take our lives back, and return to the old, self-fueled variety of Christian experience. I really do wonder why that is.

The Serenity of the Surrendered Life

Must we wait until we're desperate before we'll trust him? No! The serenity of the surrendered life is available to us every day: good ones, bad ones, and in-between ones. When we are tired of trying to be good enough and strong enough and together enough, when we are tired of juggling the complexities and struggling against the tides of confusion, when we are ready to stop the striving and receive the gift . . . Jesus is there.

Our job is simply to believe that he is who the Bible says he is: the only begotten Son of God the Father who is at one with God himself (see John 1:14,18; 10:30). Our job is to believe that he means to do what he has promised: to save us and give us a new and more abundant life (see John 3:16; 10:10).

And then, once we believe, we have only to let go. To yield. To surrender. To say, "Jesus, I quit. I'm no good at this. I can't be like you. I can't be simple or serene or loving on my own. I can't get it together or sort it out. But oh, Lord, I believe there is a better and simpler life *in* you—and I want that life. I want to be able to live the way you're calling me to live. So forgive all of my sins and failures. [Tell him what they are.] Now please come and let your Holy Spirit be the power by which I live and love. Come, Lord, and dwell in me."

This is not a fancy prayer, but Jesus will answer it. To the extent that we will let him, he really will come and live out his life in us. I know, because I see him there every day in so many of the people I love.

In fact, after church last Tuesday night, I looked at my friend Cindy's sweet face and saw him so clearly.

"Cindy," I told her, "do you know who you look like to me? You look like Jesus in his Cindy suit."

"That's because I am," she answered.

Good, Great, More-Than-Amazing News

Allowing Jesus Christ to walk around wearing the suit of our humanity is what Romans 8 is talking about when it says that we don't have to live according to our old nature anymore, that now we can live according to his Spirit. It says we will be thinking with a Spirit mind and loving with a Spirit love. It promises that the Spirit will even search our hearts and pray through us when we don't know what to pray. It says that we can live as God's kids in his kingdom and that the life he gives us will last forever.

This is the good, great, more-than-amazing news of the gospel: that the Lord is waiting only for us to give him the chance to simplify us from the inside out. He's waiting only for us to invite him in. For Jesus is more than the powerful God who is above us. He is more than the merciful God who came to live among us. He is the God who won't be happy until he's at the very center of who we are. He is the God who longs to get under our skins—to heal us and fill us and begin to flow through us.

The simple beauty of this One who walked with fishermen and lovingly touched the skin of lepers and laughed with little children is available and waiting to be poured out in us, filling us with all the serenity and love we have been seeking. With his life at the center, we really can be simpler. All of our choices—at home, at work, at play, in our relationships, in every part and particle of our lives—can flow simply from the deep center of the One who abides there.

A Simple Faith

And as we come in the quietness to be refueled by his life in ours, we will discover what we have been yearning for all along.

We will discover, at the very center of who we are, that there really is ... a place called Simplicity.

A Brass Tacks Simplicity Plan

*A*s I contemplate the joy that can come when our nervous energies are freed up to engage in meaningful communion with God and His creation, I feel moved to strip down to basics in my life.

—John Charles Cooper

Our youngest son, Andy, is a college student, a married man of ten months, and the youth pastor at our church. One part of his church job that invariably blesses me is the little weekly column he writes for our newsletter, *The Cornerstone*. This week's column was an especially good one; it was about the difference between knowing something and doing something about what we know. Andy wrote:

> I learned a good term in my communications class—narcotizing. Narcotizing is a desensitizing process that happens as a result

of our huge mass media of television, radio, magazines, etc. A narcotized person mistakes the acquiring of knowledge about a subject with doing something about that subject. In other words, they think because they know about people starving in Africa, they are doing something about it.[1]

I believe that for many years I was "narcotized" on my journey toward Simplicity. I owned shelves of books on the subject, and I was drawn to the beauty of the lifestyle they proclaimed. But I related to those books as escapist literature. I could curl up in a cozy chair and find rest and refreshment just reading about someone else's ideas and beliefs on living a simple life, but I was not giving those ideas any expression in my own life. And though I was beginning to own some of the beliefs I was reading about, I was not putting any of those beliefs into action. It was so much easier just to read about them!

In his book *Holy Sweat*, Tim Hansel laments the fact that so many of us miss out on fully living the Christian adventure. He says it is because we've never learned to "plug our theology into our biography."[2] That was certainly true of me in my search for simplicity. I spent years developing a wonderful "theology" of simplicity, but I had never taken any steps to plug it into the "biography" of my real life.

This Brass Tacks Simplicity Plan, therefore, is designed to help you begin putting feet on your ideals and teaching them to walk around in your everyday circumstances. It is meant to help you begin plugging your own personal "theology" of simplicity into the "biography" of your real life. But this plan will not change you overnight from a complicated, overwrought, rushed, stressed individual into a serene, tranquil being. It is a very simple plan with simple parameters. It can help you, if you let it, begin to locate places in your own life that you may want to simplify and begin to take action in some of these areas.

How to Use This Plan

You can follow this Brass Tacks Plan in a number of ways. You may wish to set aside a whole day or a weekend to spend some concentrated time thinking and praying through these exercises. Or you may wish to work through the questions and exercises more slowly, spending as much time as you need on each one until you have completed it. You are the only one who knows your own preferences and limitations. Choose the time frame that best suits your temperament.

You may prefer to work through the Brass Tacks Plan alone, giving yourself plenty of privacy to answer as honestly as you can. But if you are a "people person" like me, you'll probably enjoy working through the plan with someone else.

If you are married and your spouse is in tune with your interest in the subject of simplicity, this plan can provide a wonderful opportunity for the two of you to begin looking at the quality of your life together, thinking through some ways of reducing stress and simplifying the way you live. Or if you have a good friend who shares your interest in simple living, you may choose to invite that friend to read the book and spend a "Brass Tacks" day or weekend with you brainstorming practical ways both of you can begin putting some of these ideas into practice. A third option would be to pick one day each week to study the book in a group, going through a chapter at a time. The insights and experiences pooled by a group of this kind could prove invaluable, and the group support could give you the strength you need to actually move ahead toward simpler living.

You will need the following items to work through the Brass Tacks Simplicity Plan:

A Journal and Pen. If you do not already keep a journal, begin one. Buy a fancy bound book if that appeals to you, but a plain loose-leaf or spiral notebook will do. This is the place to record your own thoughts, feelings, ideas, insights, prayers, and resolutions. Make it off-limits to all but those you choose to share it with. Keeping a journal is a wonderful way to give definition to your free-floating thoughts and prayers. With pencil or pen in hand, you will find your ideas becoming clearer and your plans becoming more accessible. As you prayerfully work through the Brass Tacks Simplicity Plan, you will be amazed at the wisdom that will come to you from the tip of your very own pen!

Your Bible. Each section of the study guide suggests one or two "simplicity Scriptures" to look up . . . to help you get God's slant on simplicity. You will also want to have your Bible with you for further reading and meditation. Use a good modern translation that puts God's wisdom into plain language.

A Place Called Simplicity. This book will be your text for working through the Brass Tacks Plan.

With journal, pen, Bible, and book in hand; with a time frame, a place to work, and someone to work with (if that is your preference), you are almost ready to go! Before beginning, however, take the time to commit your journey toward simplicity to the Lord in prayer. Praise him for the beauty and simplicity of his life. Confess to him that you desire a simpler life, one more in line with his own. Ask him for the guidance and the counsel of his Holy Spirit as you proceed. Finally, ask him for the courage and the perseverance to follow through on what you discover and decide.

THE BRASS TACKS SIMPLICITY PLAN

Chapter 1: A Step Toward Simplicity

Blessed is the person who wants growth so badly that he refuses to shrink from the process that produces it.[3]

—David Swartz

❦

Simplicity Scriptures: Look up Isaiah 66:12,13 and John 14:27 and copy these verses into your journal. What do they say to you about simplifying your life?

Simplicity Suggestions:

- Turn back to the preface of the book. Answer the questions it raises, noting in your journal which answers indicate your desire for a simpler life and which areas they relate to. (For instance, a positive answer on the question about your work space and your calendar might indicate a need for less clutter and more organization in your home and office.)

- Write out a brief statement of why you desire more simplicity and in what areas. Put in any specifics that will make your statement clearer and more compelling. If you wish, share your findings with your simplicity partner or group.

- Think of times in the past when you have tried to simplify your life. (This might include small efforts, such as cleaning out a closet, or large ones, such as quitting a job.) Record your memories in your journal. What was the result of these efforts, both long and short term? Why do you think things worked out the way they did?

- Write out in twenty-five words or more why you believe that simplifying your life is not only desirable but possible. (Before you will ever start out in the direction of a place called Simplicity, you must first believe you can actually get there. Make a good case for it!) If you wish, compare answers with your partner or group.

Chapter 2: Homesick for Eden

Nature sides with grace. We are pressed from above by grace and from below by nature. We are squeezed into the Kingdom. . . . When you say Yes to Jesus Christ, the universe says Yes to you.[4]

—E. Stanley Jones

Simplicity Scripture: Look up Romans 8:22,23 and copy these verses into your notebook. What insights can you find here about simplicity?

Simplicity Suggestions:

- Suppose you could design your very own modern-day Garden of Eden with you starring in one of the leading roles. Describe in your notebook what you think your garden would be like. (Use your imagination and make it tranquil, beautiful, and serene.) What elements of this imaginary garden would you really like to incorporate into your everyday life?

- List the four losses that we humans experienced when we left the Garden. Beside each one, jot down instances when you have felt this loss in your own life. Which of the four losses do you feel most deeply?

- Have you noticed a loss of moral boundaries in our country—in movies, television, news stories? In what ways has this loss most affected the simplicity of your own life (your home life, social life, job)? Explain your answer. How would you like to remedy that loss?

- What temptations tend to pull you away from simplicity? Make a list of four or five in your notebook. What is the best way to overcome these temptations?

Chapter 3: Clearing the Cluttered Path

The last of human freedoms is the ability to choose one's attitude.[5]

—Viktor Frankel

--- ✿ ---

Simplicity Scripture: Look up Matthew 7:13,14 and copy these verses into your notebook. Consider how they apply to the issue of choosing simplicity.

Simplicity Suggestions:

- In what ways can you see that your own choices have contributed to the confusion and chaos around you? What kinds of choices could you make instead to bring more simplicity, serenity, and order into your work, home, relationships, and other areas of your life?

- Try a simple action plan. Write down three specific ways you can choose simplicity this week (in your wardrobe? in your shopping habits? in your schedule?). Pencil these choices into your calendar.

- What do you think the organizing principle of your life is? (Think about what is, not what ought to be!) Is this principle contributing to the serenity and order of your lifestyle?

- What changes would you have to make in your life to make Christ and his will the organizing principle? Discuss this decision with your partner or group.

Chapter 4: In Its Own Sweet Time

Seeing that you have to do more than have time, save time, kill time; that flowers have an action and that you can be as well as become, can measure depth as well as space, and that it is not enough to take an idiot around the world at four hundred miles an hour if he remains the same idiot when you bring him back to Main Street.[6]

—Meridel Le Sueur

Simplicity Scriptures: Look up 2 Corinthians 6:2 and Matthew 6:34. What do these two verses suggest to you about time?

Simplicity Suggestions:

- Turn back to chapter 4 and reread the descriptions of *kairos* moments. Can you remember one moment in your own life when you felt you were not being governed by the clock or the calendar? If you can, describe it in detail. Or describe a *kairos* moment you would *like* to have.

- Look at your appointment calendar or "to do" list for next week. Put stars by some of the commitments that might enable you to bring more *kairos* kinds of moments into the *chronos* of your day. (For example, you can really listen to the people you will be meeting with and try to see Christ in them.)

- Pray and ask God to bring more meaning into your time this week. Tell him that you will be open to his agenda this week. Then schedule at least one block of time for a *kairos* possibility—a Saturday morning in the park? an evening drive in the country? a long lunch with a dear friend?

Chapter 5: The House We Call Home

Home interprets heaven. Home is heaven for beginners.[7]

—Charles H. Parkhurst

Simplicity Scripture: Look up Luke 14:12,13 and copy it into your notebook. What insights about simple homes do you find there?

Simplicity Suggestions:

- In your notebook, write down the qualities of "simple homes" that are listed and described in chapter 5. Which of these qualities do you feel your house has? Which does your house lack? Write down three specific steps you could take to make your house more simple and welcoming.

- Think of several homes you have enjoyed visiting. What was it about those homes that made you feel good? In your journal, try to describe the qualities that made you feel so comfortable and welcome. In what ways could your home become more like those homes you have enjoyed?

- What takes place in your house that causes guests to leave feeling better than when they arrived? (Are they affirmed, encouraged, well-fed?) On the basis of what you discover, write down your idea of what ministry your house might have. Ask the Lord to confirm this or to show you another area of ministry you haven't thought of.

- Make a short list of the qualities you would most like your home to have (more order? better cooking? better communication? an "open heart" to guests?). Choose the one whose lack causes you the most stress at present. Write your choice at the top of your calendar for next week. Then pencil in three specific things you can do to begin working on that one quality. (For instance, "more order" might require that you start by cleaning out your own clothes closet.)

Chapter 6: Money, Malls, and Moth Teeth

We know that well-being is not defined by wealth, and so we can hold all things lightly—owning without treasuring, possessing without being possessed. We use money within the confines of a properly disciplined spiritual life, and we manage money for the glory of God and the good of all people.[8]

—Richard J. Foster

❧

Simplicity Scripture: Write down 2 Corinthians 9:7; Philippians 4:11,12; and 1 Timothy 6:17 in your notebook and consider what these verses say about financial simplicity.

Simplicity Suggestions:

- Try the exercise described in the chapter. Make a

thorough list of all your possessions and assets—write down everything you can think of! Then acknowledge God's ownership and your loanership by writing out a statement deeding these things to God. Sign the statement and keep it in your Bible or safety deposit box.

- Make another list of everything you owe—not only what the monthly payments are, but the amount it would take to pay off the debt. Ask God how he would have you deal with these commitments. You may also choose to seek counsel from a trusted friend, relative, or associate.

- Try going on a "spending diet" for a week. See if you can stay out of stores, catalogs, and restaurants. How difficult was it? What did your experience tell you about the role that spending plays in your life?

- Consider whether there is one weekly or monthly expense you can give up so you can spend that money instead on some good cause. What would you give up? On what would you spend it? Why? When . . . ?

Chapter 7: The Uncluttered Career

The only cure for the love of power is the power of love.[9]

—Sherri McAdam

❦

Simplicity Scripture: Look up Colossians 3:23,24 and write it down. What is the message for you about simplifying your work?

Simplicity Suggestions:

- Create a special section in your journal for your work. (If your job is homemaking, remember that it counts, too!) On one page of this work section, list the specific aspects of your job that complicate your life the most (the hours? the physical environment? the people?). On the next three or four pages, write the names of three or four coworkers, the ones with whom you have the most contac. Finally, make a list of four or five specific challenges you are facing at work this month.

- Use this work section as a guide for a special prayer session every day for the next week (or longer). Pray about the issues and the challenges. Pray for your coworkers by name. Ask God to make your place of work a place of peace and harmony. Record answers to prayers or changes that seem evident to you beside each item listed in your journal.

- Study the mission statement written out for a teacher on page 124. Using it as a guide, write out a mission statement for your own job. Ask the Lord to reveal to you the ministry aspects of your work. (These do not need to be specifically "spiritual" things. Any way that your positive attitude could encourage another person, for instance, would constitute ministry.) You may wish to have this simplicity document printed or hand-lettered and framed so that you can refer to it frequently.

- Find someone you admire and ask that person how he or she decreases stress and adds serenity to his or her work day. Keep a record in your journal of ideas that seem to apply to you. Can you find specific ways to make them work in your particular situation?

We are constantly gifted with a stream of "little things" which can help restore our mental and emotional balance and provide us with a rich resource for happiness—if we learn to appreciate them.[10]

—Dr. Archibald D. Hart

— ❦ —

Simplicity Scriptures: Look up Mark 6:31. Copy this verse into your notebook. What was Jesus's attitude about rest and leisure?

Simplicity Suggestions:

- Write down some reasons you think truly "restful rest" is hard to come by in our culture. What factors in your life (if any) make it difficult for you to relax and recreate?

- Review the simple pleasures described in this chapter, then try to come up with a list of activities that might help you enjoy wholesome leisure. What special opportunities for re-creation are available to you in your particular setting (city, town, country)? What kinds of simple activities do you enjoy doing—what energizes you, relaxes you, and seems delightful to you? What activities have you never tried but think you might like to try? Brainstorm about fifteen or twenty possibilities.

- Read through the list of ideas and possibilities you have made. Pick five of these activities and consider how you would make space in your life and your schedule for them. Record any "yes, but" objections that pop up in your mind—reasons you "just couldn't" fit those activities in.

- Choose at least one idea from your list and make an appointment to do it within the next month. Set aside the time you think it will take, then add an hour on either side. (It might feel artificial or even sinful to schedule "down time" like this, but sometimes it is the only way.)

- Experiment with the idea of just "being" in God's presence. Find a quiet place, a comfortable chair, and a free moment. Ask not to be disturbed. Commit this time to the Lord and then just rest in him. Give yourself permission to stop doing. Practice feeling valuable without achieving anything. Then, after twenty or thirty minutes, record your reaction. Were you nervous? Distracted? Try this exercise several times over the next few days.

Chapter 9: A Childlike Heart

A mark was on him from the day's delight, so that all his life when April was a thin green and the flavor of rain was on his tongue, an old wound would throb and a nostalgia would fill him for something he could not quite remember. A whippoorwill called across the bright night, and suddenly he was asleep. [11]

—Marjorie Kinnan Rawlings

Simplicity Scripture: Look up Matthew 18:3,4 and 5:5 and copy these verses down in your journal. What is Jesus saying here about simplicity?

Simplicity Suggestions:

- Write out three childlike qualities you feel you may have lost touch with and would like to recover (spontaneity? laughter? sensitivity? energy?). Then find a

A Brass Tacks Simplicity Plan

picture of yourself as a child. Tuck it into your Bible Whenever you encounter it during Scripture reading or prayer time, ask God to help you know how to come to him as a little child.

- In your journal list some of the things you remember about yourself as a child—ways you celebrated life, or times you felt hurt or rejected. Then, during your prayer time, give any unresolved guilt or anger to the Lord. Remember, God accepts and loves you in spite of the ways that the world might have hurt or rejected you. God desires that you live in a deeper awareness of your Father-child relationship with him.

- The Bible tells us that we may come boldly before the throne of grace without fear or hesitation. Father God wants to spend time with you, his precious child. He lovingly welcomes you and listens. What do you want to tell him? What do you want to ask him? What do you think he would like to say to you today, and what is your response? Share these things in prayer with him, and record some of them in your journal.

- This week take time to be more joyful and childlike. God encourages us to cast all our cares on him, as a little child trusts his or her father. So give yourself permission to be more childlike.

Chapter 10: A Simple Faith

> *It is a difficult lesson to learn today—to leave one's friends and family and deliberately practice the art of solitude for an hour or a day or a week. For me, the break is the most difficult. . . . And yet, once it is done, I find there is a quality to being alone that is incredibly precious. Life rushes back into the void, richer, more vivid, fuller than before.*[12]
> —Anne Morrow Lindbergh

A Brass Tacks Simplicity Plan

The remarkable thing however is that sitting in the presence of God for one hour each morning—day after day, week after week, month after month—in total confusion and with myriad distractions radically changes my life. God, who loves me so much that he sent his only son not to condemn me but to save me, does not leave me waiting in the dark too long. I might think that each hour is useless, but after thirty or sixty or ninety such useless hours, I gradually realize that I was not as alone as I thought; a very small, gentle voice has been speaking to me far beyond my noisy place.[13]

—Henri Nouwen

❧

Simplicity Scripture: Look up and write down Matthew 11:28-30. What does this verse say about simplifying the very center of your life?

Simplicity Suggestions:

- If you are not doing this already, make a commitment to have a quiet time with the Lord every day. If this seems hard because of children or work or your own inner reluctance, tell the Lord in prayer that having a quiet time is the desire of your heart and ask him earnestly to find a time and place each day. He will make a way for you.

- If spending time with God seems like one more thing to do in an overstuffed day, try some deliberate attitude adjustment. First, forcibly eject the shoulds and the oughts from your quiet time and remind yourself you are keeping an appointment with a treasured friend. Go to him with expectation and hope instead of guilt, and see what a difference it can make. You may also find it helpful to make your prayer closet as inviting as possible—with a

A Brass Tacks Simplicity Plan

scented candle, a special chair, a cozy afghan, a tape or CD playing quiet music. These physical reminders of God's beauty and presence do not bring God any nearer—he's already close—but they may help you want to be with him.

- Ask God to make your heart "a place called Simplicity" all day long today. Try to be aware of his presence with you—above you, beside you, within you. Invite him to share your day. You may even want to set up some physical reminders of his presence. Set a place for him at the table. Pull up a chair for him when you are working. Picture him there at your meetings, in the checkout line at the grocery store, as you bathe a child or cook a meal. Experience the calming difference his presence can make.

A Brass Tacks Simplicity Plan

Epilogue
Finding the Deep Currents

*T*hose who say, What can I do? must know the answer. It is, give away all you have, and follow me. This means giving up conformity, the current system, the good opinion of the world, the easy reliance on custom. It means living imaginatively, aggressively, recklessly, enduring hardships to a degree.[1]

—Harlan Hubbard

There was a picture on our dining room wall when I was a child that always fascinated me. It was a small black-and-white etching of a trapeze act. In it, a female trapeze artist had just let go of her swing with one hand and was reaching out with the other for the hand of the man who was to catch her. The picture captured the precise moment in which the woman was suspended in midair with no support, like a great, graceful seabird above an ocean of terrified faces. As I stared at that picture as a child, I could never quite decide whether I was looking at a woman getting ready to fall to her death, or a woman just about to achieve some great, adventurous acrobatic feat.

Our journey toward a simpler life has felt like that to me many times over the past year and a half. It has been a journey of letting go and taking hold. Letting go of what felt safe, and reaching out to take hold of the unknown. At times I haven't known whether I was flying or falling, whether I was doing something brave and beautiful or preparing for a colossal crash.

Perhaps all journeys of any substance are about letting go and taking hold. Perhaps all change is simply a process of releasing something that is familiar and reaching out for something that is new. And maybe that is why change can be so difficult—because in that process there will inevitably be those "midair moments" when the old has been released but the new has not yet been seized and we are suspended somewhere in the middle.

A Midair Moment

I had a mild midair moment only yesterday. Our son, Andy, brought a carload of his friends over from Mobile to canoe and swim, to barbecue and play guitars, and just generally to enjoy a change of scene. We had a wonderful day. But as it got later and later and their going back to town seemed less and less likely, I began to wonder where we would find room in this tiny cabin for all these folks to lay their heads. Suddenly I found myself missing my house back in town will all its spare bedrooms and bathrooms and square feet. Suddenly, for just a moment, I was suspended somewhere between my old life and my new one, out in midair.

But my midair moment was short-lived, thank goodness. Sofas were spoken for, beds were grabbed, roll-up mats were retrieved from the storeroom, and soon our herd of happy guests was snugly settled under a patchwork assortment of spreads and sheets. No one seemed to mind being parked wherever there was a space on the floor. Everyone slept comfortably and late.

This morning we shared a leisurely breakfast of cinnamon toast and coffee with Andy and his friends before hugging each one and sending them on their way.

My brief midair moment last night was just another step in the letting-go-and-taking-hold process. I was able to see, once the moment had passed, how many things in our old life that I once considered "standard equipment" were really just "optional features." I was able to seize with a firm grasp the reality that simple things suffice when our hearts are content.

A Seven-Year Drift

Naturalist and artist Harlan Hubbard found great contentment in his simple lifestyle, though few of his contemporaries understood him. When he built a small but sturdy shanty boat on the banks of the Ohio River, and pushed off with his scant supplies and his wife, Anna, for a seven-year drift on the inland waterways of the United States, he was regarded by his neighbors as eccentric, to say the least. But as he let go of land and allowed his boat to find the currents of the river, he felt himself becoming part of something new and lovely and life-changing.

Biographer Wendell Berry said of Hubbard's journey:

> He wanted to drift on the river not so much to see where it went as to be one with it, to go with it as virtually part of it. He wished perhaps to live out a kind of parable. . . . In drifting, one must accept a severe limitation upon one's intentions. But in giving oneself to the currents, in thus subordinating one's intentions, one becomes eligible for unintended goods, unwished-for gifts—and often these goods and gifts surpass those that one had intended or wished for.[2]

This journey (Spike's and mine) has been that kind of a parable for me. I have purposed to let go of my own driven, often frantic agenda in order to find and be moved by the deep, strong currents of God's will for my life.

I really didn't know what I would find on this journey, and I'm still not exactly certain. It may take many years to fully understand what God is working out in me. I do know that I have died a little. I have lost my life to find it. I have let go of one kind of life to take hold of another. I have struggled with (and still at times struggle with) loneliness and the pain of changing. I have prayed through anxiety and boredom and the desire at times to jump ship and swim back to shore. But I am finding that as I continue to let go, the deep currents of God are moving me daily into places of quiet beauty. And the "unwished-for gifts," the unexpected treasures I am drawing from these deep waters, are satisfying and sweet.

You are on a different journey. Different because it is your own. You can't be sure exactly what you will find either. But I want to encourage you not to turn back, not to jump ship, though you may feel like it at times. Though the going may sometimes be ragged and choppy, the destination is going to be worth the struggle for both of us. I feel it. This hunger in our hearts for a saner, simpler place is part of the evidence that such a place exists. God has put this hunger in us to draw us to himself, his way, his kingdom, his Son. And when we finally become one with the river of his will, we'll look up one day, you and I, to see that we're home. Finally home. Drifting gently ashore at a beautiful landing called Simplicity.

Finding the Deep Currents

Notes

Chapter 1—A Step Toward Simplicity
1. A phrase coined by Nora Ephron.
2. Archibald D. Hart, *The Hidden Link between Adrenalin and Stress: The Exciting New Breakthrough That Helps You Overcome Stress Damage* (Waco, TX: Word, 1981).
3. Richard Foster, *The Freedom of Simplicity* (San Francisco: Harper, 1981), v.
4. Henry David Thoreau, quoted in David Shi, *In Search of the Simple Life* (Salt Lake City: Peregrine Smith Books, 1986), 171.

Chapter 2—Homesick for Eden
1. From "Homesick For Eden," lyric by Claire Cloninger and music by Paul Smith, © Word, Inc., 1989.
2. Pat Conroy, *The Prince of Tides* (Boston: Houghton Mifflin, 1986), 471.
3. Curtis Cloninger, "How I Stopped Worrying and Learned to Love the Truth," *The Sewanee Purple*, 28 January 1991, 9.

Chapter 3—Clearing the Cluttered Path
1. Paul Borthwick, *101 Ways to Simplify Your Life* (Wheaton, IL: Victor, 1992), 19.
2. "Author's Guide to the Good Life: Keep It Simple," *Pensacola News Journal*, 12 April 1993, D-1.
3. Sue Bender, *Plain and Simple: A Woman's Journey to the Amish* (San Francisco: Harper, 1991), 4.
4. Bender, *Plain and Simple*, 141.
5. Stephanie Winston, *Getting Organized* (New York: Norton, 1978), 25.
6. "First Things First," lyric by Claire Cloninger, music by Don Koch, © Word Music and the Benson Company, 1986.

Chapter 4—In Its Own Sweet Time
1. Claire Cloninger, "Between Two Thieves," © Word, Inc., 1991.
2. Ralph Keyes, "Do You Have the Time?" *Parade Magazine*, 16 February 1993, 21.
3. Ibid., 23.

4. David Wilkerson with John and Elizabeth Sherrill, *The Cross and the Switchblade* (Lincoln, VA: Chosen, 1963), 11.
5. Amy Saltzman, *Downshifting* (New York: Harper Perenniel, 1992), 21.
6. Karla Worley and Claire Cloninger, *When the Glass Slipper Doesn't Fit and the Silver Spoon Is in Someone Else's Mouth* (Dallas: Word, 1993), 74.

Chapter 5—The House We Call Home
1. Phyllis McGinley, *Sixpence in Her Shoe* (New York: Macmillan, 1965), 60.
2. "The House We Call Home," from *Love Will Be Our Home*, lyric by Claire Cloninger/music by Keith Christopher, © Word Music, 1991.
3. Vicki Covington, *Night Ride Home* (New York: Simon & Schuster, 1992), 27.
4. Doris Longacre, *Living More with Less* (Scottsdale, PA: Herald Press, 1980), 143.
5. Alexandra Stoddard, *Living a Beautiful Life* (New York: Random House, 1986), 4.
6. Don Aslett, *Clutter's Last Stand* (Cincinnati: Writer's Digest Books, 1984), 2-3.
7. Anne Morrow Lindbergh, *Gift from the Sea* (New York: Pantheon, 1955), 114-115.
8. Longacre, *Living More with Less*.
9. Longacre, *Living More with Less*, 120.
10. Marjorie Kinnan Rawlings, *Cross Creek* (New York: Scribner's, 1942), 3.
11. "Elixir," © Robert A. Cloninger, 1984.
12. John Burroughs, quoted in David E. Shi, *In Search of the Simple Life* (Salt Lake City: Peregrine Smith Books, 1986), 192.

Chapter 6—Money, Malls, and Moth Teeth
1. Not her real name.
2. Paul Borthwick, *101 Ways to Simplify Your Life* (Wheaton, IL: Victor, 1992), 32.
3. Foster, *The Freedom of Simplicity*, 127.
4. Patricia H. Sprinkle, *Women Who Do Too Much* (Grand Rapids, MI: Zondervan, 1992), 157.
5. For information on the Crown Ministries Group nearest you, call (407) 331-6000 or write Crown Ministries, 530 Crown Oak Center Drive, Longwood, FL 32750. Twelve-week courses are offered in most cities three times a year—January, May, and September.

6. "Introduction Notes," *Crown Ministries Small Group Financial Study* (Longwood, FL: Crown Ministries, 1986), 9.
7. Richard J. Foster, *Celebration of Discipline* (San Francisco: Harper, 1988), 86.
8. Ibid., 87.
9. "Moth Teeth," lyric by Claire Cloninger, © Word, 1988.
10. Peter Maurin, quoted in David E. Shi, *In Search of the Simple Life* (Salt Lake City: Peregrine Smith Books, 1986), 243-244.
11. "Debt," *Crown Ministries Small Group Financial Study*, 37.
12. Foster, *Freedom of Simplicity*, 127.

Chapter 7—The Uncluttered Career

1. Charles deGravelles, *The Well Governed Son* (New Orleans: New Orleans Poetry Journal Press, 1987).
2. Alexandra Stoddard, *Daring to Be Yourself* (New York: Doubleday, 1990), 182-183.
3. Sue Bender, *Plain and Simple: A Woman's Journey to the Amish* (San Francisco: Harper, 1991), 84-85.
4. Melodie Beattie, *The Language of Letting Go* (New York: Harper, 1990), 227.

Chapter 8—Pockets of Heaven on the Apron of Earth

1. Quoted in Amy Saltzman, *Downshifting* (New York: Harper Perennial, 1992), 23.
2. Barbara Holland, "The Place Called Summer," *Country Journal*, May/June 1993, 21.
3. Doris Longacre, *Living More with Less* (Scottsdale, PA: Herald, 1980), chapter 7.
4. John Hadamuscin, *Simple Pleasures* (New York: Harmony Books, 1992), 7.
5. Claire Cloninger, *Postcards from Heaven* (Dallas: Word, 1992), 94.
6. Paul Borthwick, *101 Ways to Simplify Your Life* (Wheaton, IL: Victor, 1992), 68-69.
7. Robert Cloninger, unpublished journal, 16 October 1983.
8. Wendell Berry, "II," *Sabbaths* (San Francisco: North Point Press, 1987), 8.

Chapter 9—A Childlike Heart

1. Robert Cloninger, unpublished journal, 12 July 1993.
2. Tim Hansel, *Holy Sweat* (Waco, TX: Word, 1987), 143.
3. Henri J.M. Nouwen, *The Road to Daybreak* (New York: Doubleday, 1988), 11.
4. Margery Williams, *The Velveteen Rabbit* (New York: Doubleday, 1958), 17, 20.

5. Claire Cloninger, "Precious Child," *Christmas Is Calling You Home* (Dallas: Word, 1991).

Chapter 10—A Simple Faith

1. Foster, *Celebration of Discipline*, 5.
2. Gerhardt Tersteegen, quoted in G.H. Morling, *The Quest for Serenity*, ed. Ruth Bell Graham (Dallas: Word, 1989), 12.
3. Bernard of Clairvaux, quoted in Jean Fleming, *Between Walden and the Whirlwind* (Colorado Springs: NavPress, 1985), 22.
4. Fleming, *Between Walden and the Whirlwind*, 23.
5. Oswald Chambers, *My Utmost for His Highest* (Westwood, NJ: Barbour, 1935 and 1963), 171.
6. "Right Where We Are" © Claire Cloninger, 1993.
7. Brother Lawrence of the Resurrection, *The Practice of the Presence of God* (New York: Walker, 1974), 37.

A Brass Tacks Simplicity Plan

1. Andy Cloninger, "The Media or the Maker," *The Cornerstone* (newsletter produced for Christ Church, Mobile, Alabama), 12 May 1993, 8.
2. Tim Hansel, *Holy Sweat* (Waco, TX: Word, 1987), 26.
3. David Swartz, *Dancing with Broken Bones* (Colorado Springs: NavPress, 1987), 82.
4. E. Stanley Jones, *The Divine Yes* (Nashville: Abingdon, 1975), 53-54.
5. Viktor Frankel, quoted in Ed Wheat and Gloria Okes Perkins, *Secret Choices* (Grand Rapids, MI: Pyranee Books, 1989), 21.
6. Meridel Le Sueur, *North Star Country* (New York: Duell, Sloan and Pearce, 1945), 185.
7. Charles H. Parkhurst, quoted in *Quotation Dictionary* (Little Falls, NJ: Career Publishing, 1984), 139.
8. Richard J. Foster, *Money, Sex, and Power* (San Francisco: Harper & Row, 1985), 72.
9. Sherri McAdam, quoted in Foster, *Money, Sex, and Power*, 196.
10. Thomas Howard, *Christ the Tiger* (Philadelphia: Lippencott, 1967), 157.
11. Marjorie Kinnan Rawlings, *The Yearling* (New York: Scribner's, 1938), 14-15.
12. Anne Morrow Lindbergh, *Gift from the Sea* (New York: Pantheon, 1955 and 1975), 42.
13. Henri J. M. Nouwen, *The Road to Daybreak* (New York: Doubleday, 1988), 30.

Finding the Deep Currents

1. Wendell Berry, *Harlan Hubbard: Life and Work* (Lexington, KY: The University Press of Kentucky, 1990), 39.

2. Ibid., 16.

Other Good
Harvest House Reading

THE SPIRIT OF LOVELINESS
by *Emilie Barnes*

Join Emilie Barnes as she shares insights into the inner qualities of spiritual beauty and explores the places of the heart where true femininity is born. With hundreds of "lovely" ideas to help you personalize your home, Emilie shows that beauty *can* be achieved with even the lightest touch of creativity. Your spirit of loveliness will shine through as you make your home a place of prayer, peace, and pleasure for your family.

MEETING GOD IN QUIET PLACES
by *F. LaGard Smith*

When the clamor of life threatens to overwhelm you, come share a quiet moment of peaceful intimacy with the Father in *Meeting God in Quiet Places*. These 30 sensitive parables from nature, drawn from bestselling author F. LaGard Smith's reflections in the Cotswold region of England, will refresh both your eye and soul. With illustrative pencil-sketch drawings by English artist Glenda Rae, this special book is one you'll return to throughout the year for life-renewing insights to guide you to the very heart of God.

NEAR TO THE HEART OF GOD
by *Deborah Kern*

God wants us to pray. And He created prayer in such a way that a consistent, life-changing prayer experience would not be out of anyone's reach. Deborah Kern's thoughtful chapters and down-to-earth illustrations shed light on even the hard-to-understand aspects of prayer, including prayers that go unanswered and what to do when you just can't pray. Wherever you are in prayer—whether you've been praying for years or are just starting out—this book will bring freshness and renewed enthusiasm to your prayer life.

QUIET TIMES FOR COUPLES
by *H. Norman Wright*

Noted counselor and author Norm Wright provides the help you need to nurture your oneness in Christ. In a few moments together each day you will discover a deeper, richer intimacy with each other and with God, sharing your fondest dreams and deepest thoughts—creating memories of quiet times together.

Dear Reader:

We would appreciate hearing from you regarding this Harvest House nonfiction book. It will enable us to continue to give you the best in Christian publishing.

1. What most influenced you to purchase *A Place Called Simplicity*?
   - ☐ Author
   - ☐ Subject matter
   - ☐ Backcover copy
   - ☐ Recommendations
   - ☐ Cover/Title
   - ☐ _____

2. Where did you purchase this book?
   - ☐ Christian bookstore
   - ☐ General bookstore
   - ☐ Department store
   - ☐ Grocery store
   - ☐ Other

3. Your overall rating of this book:
   - ☐ Excellent ☐ Very good ☐ Good ☐ Fair ☐ Poor

4. How likely would you be to purchase other books by this author?
   - ☐ Very likely
   - ☐ Somewhat likely
   - ☐ Not very likely
   - ☐ Not at all

5. What types of books most interest you?
   (check all that apply)
   - ☐ Women's Books
   - ☐ Marriage Books
   - ☐ Current Issues
   - ☐ Christian Living
   - ☐ Bible Studies
   - ☐ Fiction
   - ☐ Biographies
   - ☐ Children's Books
   - ☐ Youth Books
   - ☐ Other _____

6. Please check the box next to your age group.
   - ☐ Under 18
   - ☐ 18-24
   - ☐ 25-34
   - ☐ 35-44
   - ☐ 45-54
   - ☐ 55 and over

Mail to: Editorial Director
Harvest House Publishers
1075 Arrowsmith
Eugene, OR 97402

Name _____

Address _____

City _____ State _____ Zip _____

**Thank you for helping us to help you
in future publications!**